Succeed or Sink

CHANDOS
ASIAN STUDIES SERIES:
CONTEMPORARY ISSUES AND TRENDS

Series Editor: Professor Chris Rowley,
Centre for Research on Asian Management, Cass Business School,
City University, UK;
HEAD Foundation, Singapore
(e-mail: c.rowley@city.ac.uk)

Chandos Publishing is pleased to publish this major Series of books entitled *Asian Studies: Contemporary Issues and Trends*. The Series Editor is Professor Chris Rowley, Director, Centre for Research on Asian Management, City University, UK and Director, Research and Publications, HEAD Foundation, Singapore.

Asia has clearly undergone some major transformations in recent years and books in the Series examine this transformation from a number of perspectives: economic, management, social, political and cultural. We seek authors from a broad range of areas and disciplinary interests: covering, for example, business/management, political science, social science, history, sociology, gender studies, ethnography, economics and international relations, etc.

Importantly, the Series examines both current developments and possible future trends. The Series is aimed at an international market of academics and professionals working in the area. The books have been specially commissioned from leading authors. The objective is to provide the reader with an authoritative view of current thinking.

New authors: we would be delighted to hear from you if you have an idea for a book. We are interested in both shorter, practically orientated publications (45,000+ words) and longer, theoretical monographs (75,000–100,000 words). Our books can be single, joint or multi-author volumes. If you have an idea for a book, please contact the publishers or Professor Chris Rowley, the Series Editor.

Dr Glyn Jones
Chandos Publishing
E-mail: gjones@chandospublishing.com
www.chandospublishing.com

Professor Chris Rowley
Cass Business School, City University
E-mail: c.rowley@city.ac.uk
www.cass.city.ac.uk/faculty/c.rowley

Chandos Publishing: Chandos Publishing is an imprint of Woodhead Publishing Limited. The aim of Chandos Publishing is to publish books of the highest possible standard: books that are both intellectually stimulating and innovative.

We are delighted and proud to count our authors from such well known international organisations as the Asian Institute of Technology, Tsinghua University, Kookmin University, Kobe University, Kyoto Sangyo University, London School of Economics, University of Oxford, Michigan State University, Getty Research Library, University of Texas at Austin, University of South Australia, University of Newcastle, Australia, University of Melbourne, ILO, Max-Planck Institute, Duke University and the leading law firm Clifford Chance.

A key feature of Chandos Publishing's activities is the service it offers its authors and customers. Chandos Publishing recognises that its authors are at the core of its publishing ethos, and authors are treated in a friendly, efficient and timely manner. Chandos Publishing's books are marketed on an international basis, via its range of overseas agents and representatives.

Professor Chris Rowley: Dr Rowley, BA, MA (Warwick), DPhil (Nuffield College, Oxford) is the founding Director of the *Centre for Research on Asian Management* and Research Professor at Cass Business School, City University, London, UK (*http://www.cass.city.ac.uk/research-and-faculty/centres/cram*). He has acted as an advisor to the *HEAD Foundation*, Singapore and is its Director of Research and Publications, helping to establish its Think Tank. He is Editor of the *Asia Pacific Business Review* (*http://www.tandf.co.uk/journals/titles/13602381.asp*), Book Series Editor of both *Working in Asia* and *Asian Studies* and serves on many Editorial Boards. He is well known and highly regarded in the area, with visiting appointments at leading Asian universities and Editorial Boards in the UK, Asia and the US. He has given various talks and lectures at universities, companies and organisations internationally with research and consultancy experience with unions, and business and government; his previous employment includes varied work in both the public and private sectors. Professor Rowley has published widely and researches on a range of areas including international and comparative human resource management and Asia Pacific management and business. He has been awarded grants from the British Academy, an ESRC AIM International Study Fellowship and gained a 5-year RCUK Fellowship in Asian Business and Management. He acts as a reviewer for many funding bodies, as well as numerous journals and publishers. Professor Rowley publishes extensively, including in leading US and UK journals, with over 400 articles, books and chapters and other contributions in practitioner outlets as well as knowledge transfer engagement and international radio and newspaper interviews.

Bulk orders: some organisations buy a number of copies of our books. If you are interested in doing this, we would be pleased to discuss a discount. Please contact on e-mail wp@woodheadpublishing.com or telephone +44 (0) 1223 499140.

Succeed or Sink

Business sustainability under globalisation

CHRIS ROWLEY,
JAYANTEE MUKHERJEE SAHA
AND DAVID ANG

CP
CHANDOS
PUBLISHING

Oxford Cambridge Philadelphia New Delhi

Chandos Publishing
Hexagon House
Avenue 4
Station Lane
Witney
Oxford OX28 4BN
UK
Tel: +44 (0) 1993 848726
E-mail: info@chandospublishing.com
www.chandospublishing.com

Chandos Publishing is an imprint of Woodhead Publishing Limited

Woodhead Publishing Limited
80 High Street
Sawston
Cambridge CB22 3HJ
UK
Tel: +44 (0) 1223 499140
Fax: +44 (0) 1223 832819
www.woodheadpublishing.com

First published in 2012

ISBN: 978-0-08-101728-9 (print) (Chandos Publishing)
ISBN: 978-0-85709-166-6 (print) (Woodhead Publishing)
ISBN: 978-1-78063-331-2 (online)

© C. Rowley, J. M. Saha and D. Ang, 2012

British Library Cataloguing-in-Publication Data.
A catalogue record for this book is available from the British Library.

Typeset by RefineCatch Limited, Bungay, Suffolk
Printed in the UK and USA.

To Mr S. Huang in sincere recognition of our friendship and also your support for human capital development in Asia.

Contents

List of figures and tables

Figures

Tables

Foreword

Dave Ulrich

In the marketplace for business ideas, every few years an idea goes viral and shifts how people think and act in business settings. These ideas have included quality, strategy (called strategery by one American leader), vision/mission/values and globalisation. Recently, pressures for social responsibility have led many in business to seriously consider the concept of sustainability. As with other viral ideas, the concept starts simple and then becomes increasingly broad and complex. Business sustainability started with a need for businesses to participate in managing their social responsibility, primarily their carbon footprint. As the idea has evolved, it has broadened to a concern for the triple bottom line of people, prosperity and planet.

When the ideas spin out of control and risk becoming meaningless because they are so pervasive that they mean everything to everyone, it is very important to recalibrate the premise behind an idea. Rowley, Saha and Ang in this book take stock of the multiple dimensions of business sustainability and synthesise how this broadening idea may be focused and useful.

One of the strengths of this book is not only capturing the essence of sustainability, but also demonstrating how it applies in an exciting and rapidly emerging economy – Singapore.

Anyone who has visited Singapore recognises the vitality and energy of this diverse and growing city state. The city state is characterised by political stability (the popularised don't chew gum legacy symbolises control and safety), modern skyscrapers (a trade centre bridging East and West), diversity (one Christmas holiday we noticed the Buddhists playing Christmas carols), and a stylish economy (my wife and I recently counted about 40 per cent jewellery stores in one of their new malls – in America 40 per cent of mall space is probably food). Yet behind this modern miracle are rich traditions and real disciplines.

Political and business leaders in Singapore recognise that human capital is their primary asset, so they invest heavily in it. Parents work to educate their children. Leaders invest in their employees. Government establishes knowledge centres and universities in leadership and talent. People treat other people with enormous respect. Social differences are accepted and respected. My visits to Singapore have established not only professional colleagues but personal friends.

And, Singapore business works. It balances the vision for a future with enormous attention to detail. One quick example: almost anyone who travels often can quickly appreciate why the Singapore airport (Changi Airport Group) has dominated airport awards for the last decade. Even casual passengers know that the airport works, with an emphasis on efficiency, service, and responsiveness. Behind this success is a management team enormously committed to the detail. They recently recognised that the bathroom cleanliness might shape the image of the overall airport experience, so they put in passenger triggered electronic monitors that would signal untidy bathrooms and assigned a rapid response team to clean these targeted restrooms. This attention to detail ties to their vision for the overall airport.

So, into this remarkable setting, Rowley, Saha and Ang synthesise what defines business sustainability. Their historical overview of sustainability offers context for the idea. Their research into a mix of small to large Singaporean companies helps demonstrate how leaders think about sustainability. Their conclusions help codify how future leaders might increase sustainability in their organisations. One of their interesting findings is that the largest reason for lack of sustainability is leadership (80 per cent) so their book should . . . and does . . . inform leaders on how they can increase sustainability.

When I read their interviews, I was struck by how business sustainability requires the management of a number of paradoxes:

- Inside and outside: sustainability started with attention to the carbon footprint and social responsibility but has shifted to people and organisation actions inside a company that reinforce external sustainability;
- Big and small: sometimes leaders look for large and dramatic sustainability actions, but they need to be complemented with lots of little successes that lead to success;
- Old and new: modern technology and other actions encourage sustainability, but many of the tried and true efforts of relationships and personal touch are still essential;
- Stable and changing: while sustainability should become a stable pattern within a company, the rapid pace of change requires adjustment and learning in the short term;
- Confident and humble: leaders who build sustainability have confidence because they are doing the right thing right, but they are also humble enough to learn and listen to others;
- Hard and soft: sustainability shows up in the hard measures of business success, and also in the softer emotions of business passion;

- Past and future: by definition sustainable companies have a long legacy and history, but they constantly plan for the future.

As the authors note, these paradoxes need to be attended to as leaders build the quilt of sustainability. By so doing, these leaders attend to multiple stakeholders; they enact a balanced scorecard; and they accomplish the triple bottom line.

I recommend this book to political leaders who are charged with regulatory policies to build country sustainability, to business leaders who will see the connection between sustainability investments and investor confidence, to HR professionals who build organisation infrastructure to sustain success, and to organisation scholars who seek to understand and study how organisations evolve and respond to modern settings.

My colleague Norm Smallwood and I are working on how to build leadership sustainability. This work has already informed our thinking. My thanks to the authors for their insights and diligence.

Dave Ulrich
Alpine, Utah
USA
March 2011

Foreword

S. B. Borwankar

When I was asked to write the foreword to this book, I could hardly contain my enthusiasm. Not only was I already immersed in the subject-matter by virtue of my job, but I also saw an opportunity to summarise the last few years of acute observation and learning on a topic that is corporate sustainability.

Succeed or Sink is a unique book which provides an Asian perspective on how big and small corporate houses responded to the post-2008 global financial crisis with a broad and integrated approach towards business (3Ps). This book holds the precise nerve of the corporate sector and provides a ready-made guide of benchmark practices to be followed by corporate sectors during downturn.

I must appreciate the efforts of the authors and their extensive work on case studies pertaining to research, findings, analysis, results, conclusions, implications and guidance concerning the recent developments in the corporate world across South East Asia.

If you're a business leader, a policy-maker, or a strategist, then this is the perfect success mantra for you on how to keep your business sustainable.

S. B. Borwankar
Sr. Vice President (Manufacturing operations)
Tata Motors
India

Foreword

Sanjay Chaudhuri

It gives me great pleasure to write the foreword for this book. The book comes at an opportune time. The world is just shaking off the effects of one of the most devastating financial crisis in living memory. Companies that were decades old have vanished in the wink of an eye.

It is in times like these that one often wonders if enterprise is sustainable. Will the companies we know today be around tomorrow? Using in-depth research and case studies from organisations small and large, young and old (even over a hundred years old), the team have put together a truly integrated approach to the question of business sustainability and its challenges. The learning is at once relevant and applicable to businesses everywhere.

Here you will find hypotheses to important questions that keep some of us awake at nights. How can a business remain sustainable? Can businesses prosper for long periods of time? Is it possible to measure and predict sustainability of organisations? How can a business stay relevant? What does a sustainable future look like? And most importantly, are any lessons being learnt by organisations?

The team have taken a complex subject and researched it in a manner that is easy to understand and a pleasure to read. The mantra of the new decade will surely be 'SOS' (Succeed or Sink)!

Sanjay Chaudhuri
Global Business Director
Ogilvy & Mather Singapore

Map of South East Asia

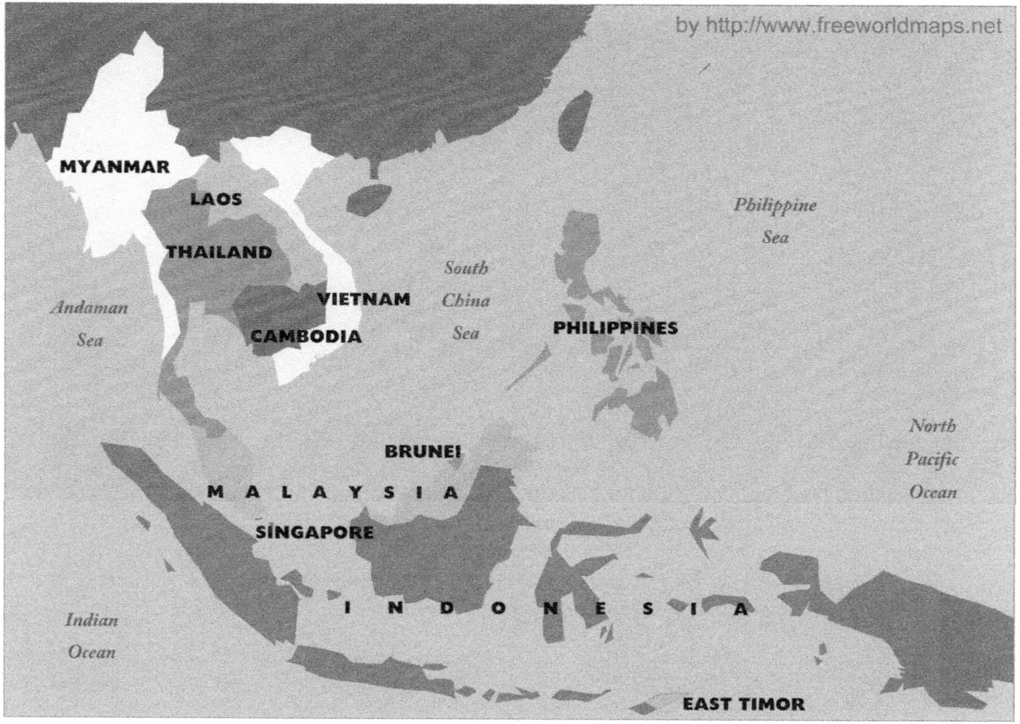

by http://www.freeworldmaps.net

North
Pacific
Ocean

Philippine
Sea

PHILIPPINES

MYANMAR

LAOS

THAILAND

VIETNAM

CAMBODIA

South
China
Sea

BRUNEI

MALAYSIA

SINGAPORE

I N D O N E S I A

EAST TIMOR

Andaman
Sea

Indian
Ocean

About the authors

Professor Rowley: Dr Rowley, BA, MA (Warwick), DPhil (Nuffield College, Oxford) is the founding Director of the *Centre for Research on Asian Management* and Research Professor at Cass Business School, City University, London, UK. He has acted as an advisor to the *HEAD Foundation*, Singapore and is its Director of Research and Publications, helping to establish its Think Tank. He is Editor of the *Asia Pacific Business Review*, Book Series Editor of both *Working in Asia* and *Asian Studies* and serves on many Editorial Boards. He is well known and highly regarded in the area, with visiting appointments at leading Asian universities and Editorial Boards in the UK, Asia and the US. He has given various talks and lectures at universities, companies and organisations internationally with research and consultancy experience with unions, and business and government; his previous employment includes varied work in both the public and private sectors. Professor Rowley has published widely and researches on a range of areas including international and comparative human resource management and Asia Pacific management and business, with over 400 articles, books and chapters and other contributions in practitioner outlets as well as knowledge transfer engagement and international radio and newspaper interviews.

Ms. Jayantee Mukherjee Saha is the Director and Principal Consultant of Aei4eiA, a Sydney-based management research and consultancy firm, and professional member of Singapore Human Resources Institute (SHRI). Prior to this, she worked as Principal Researcher at SHRI where she was responsible for leading strategic projects on pertinent human resources issues to provide solutions to stakeholders. She has extensive experience in the field of management and human resources and worked closely with Government/public sector agencies, MNCs/SMEs, global bodies, academia/professional firms in the region and beyond. She regularly writes and speaks at various forums and has over 37 publications and written a book on Management and Organizational Behaviour.

Mr. David Ang is the Executive Director at SHRI. He has extensive experience in the field of human resources and business. David was the former Secretary General and Treasurer of the World Federation of Personnel Management Associations (WFPMA) – an umbrella group that holds together human resource associations from regions across the world from May 2006 to April 2008. His leadership role as the former Chair of the 11th World HR Congress & Business-Connect Exposition won him worldwide accolades for successful execution of the largest HR event in the Asia Pacific region. David is an editorial member of the international peer refereed journal, Research and Practice in Human Resource Management (RPHRM).

Introduction: setting the context of business sustainability and globalisation

Abstract: New business infrastructure and competitive human capital within a dynamic labour market are factors that lead organisations to redefine their business strategies and enhance people management practices. Addressing these efficiently means that organisations will have to strike a balance with their limiting resources and constraints as they work towards business excellence and sustainability. This chapter introduces the context of this book and elaborates the research methodologies which are the basis of this book. It also explains why this book has a focus on Singapore and its linkage to the dynamics of business sustainability under globalisation.

Key words: human resources, Singapore, Singapore Human Resources Institute (SHRI).

Introduction

The post-2008 global financial crisis and its commensurate impacts prompted businesses around the world to re-examine their capability to be able to better survive and endure through such economic strife and chaos. Also, the term 'business sustainability' became a more popular buzzword amongst many managers and corporate boardrooms. Our book presents an Asian perspective on this area of business sustainability and it is about gaining a greater and more nuanced understanding concerning how recent developments and future actions in one part of the world have wider lessons and a global impact. As such, our findings, analysis, conclusions and implications have relevance beyond just Asia.

The book examines the topic of business sustainability from a broad and integrated approach to business. This encapsulates the '3Ps' of: people, prosperity and the planet. Furthermore, the book acknowledges the contributions and challenges for not only multinational companies (MNCs) and large organisations, but also diverse small and medium sized enterprises (SMEs) in this situation. The numerous benefits that organisations can attain with better governance, social and environmental practices, are also analysed in the following chapters. Importantly, real life cases of recent organisational events and experiences based on managerial views and comments are used. These are the result of research conducted in Singapore.

Why Singapore? Singapore is strategically located at the crossroads of two Asian superpowers – China and India – and is a major international transportation hub, positioned on many sea and air trade routes. Along with Hong Kong, Taiwan and South Korea, Singapore is one of the Asian Tiger economies. Ranked third in the World Economic Forum's Global Competitiveness Index (GCI) report 2009–10 and first among the Asian countries (WEF 2010), Singapore is somewhat representative of more developed Asia. Also, Singapore is a large, busy port and entrepot city-state with an important and leading financial centre and an economy that is based upon foreign MNC capital (Dent 2003: 255). By way of illustration, we can note that foreign transnational corporations (TNCs) accounted for well over half of Singapore's production, employment and investment and around 80 per cent of its exports by 2000 (Lim 2009: 1). Hence, the business cases, experiences and perspectives that organisations operating in Singapore have on business sustainability carry the flavours of Asia and the world, though there are also a few instances where they may be more unique, specific and context-constrained.

Singapore in context

Singapore is a cosmopolitan world city located 137 kilometers North of the equator in South East Asia between Malaysia (separated by the Straits of Johor to the North) and Indonesia (separated by the Singapore Straits to the South) covering 687 square kilometres over 60 islands and with on-going land reclamation projects. It is very densely populated, with a population of 4.7 million. Its age structure is as follows: 0–14 years old: 14.4 per cent; 15–64 years: 76.7 per cent; 65+ years: 8.9 per cent; with a median age of 39.6 years, population growth of 0.863 per cent and total fertility rate of 1.1 (CIA World Factbook 2010).

Historical and political

From the second century there are early records of settlement on the island. Known by the Javanese name of 'Temasek' ('sea town'), the island was an outpost of the Sumatran Srivijaya empire. Between the sixteenth and nineteenth centuries it was part of the Sultanate of Johor. In 1613 Portuguese raiders burnt the settlement and for the next two centuries the island remained obscure.

Singapore began in 1819, with Sir Stamford Raffles, who spotted the island's potential as a strategic trading post for South East Asia and signed a treaty to develop the Southern part of Singapore as a British trading post and settlement for the East India Company. Singapore was a territory controlled by a Malay Sultan until 1824, when it became a British possession and then, in 1826, part of the Straits Settlements – a British colony.

During the Second World War the Japanese defeated the British army. Following the war the British allowed Singapore to hold its first general election in 1955. The foundation of modern Singapore started with the formation of the People's Action Party (PAP) in 1954. Led by Lee Kuan Yew as secretary general, the party sought to attract a following among the mostly poor and non-English speaking masses. The pro-independence victory led to demands for complete self-rule and finally led to internal self-government with a prime minister and cabinet overseeing all matters of government, except for defence and foreign affairs. Elections in 1959 followed and led to a self-governing state.

Singapore declared independence and joined the Malaysian Federation in 1963 and the Republic of Singapore became an independent nation in 1965 (Lepoer 1989). Lee Kuan Yew became the first prime minister and remained so until 1990. Under the administration of Singapore's second prime minister, Goh Chok Tong, he also served as senior minister and holds the post of minister mentor, a post created when his son, Lee Hsien Loong, became Singapore's third prime minister in 2004 (*The Guardian* 2004).

Singapore is a parliamentary republic with a UK-style system of unicameral parliamentary government representing different constituencies. The PAP dominates the political process and has won control of parliament at every election since self-government. The majority of executive powers rest with the cabinet, which is headed by the prime minister. The president has a ceremonial role, although the post was granted some veto powers in 1991.

Economic

In his book, *From Third World to First: The Singapore Story 1965–2000* (Lee 2000), Lee Kuan Yew narrates how he and a small group of Singaporean leaders banded together and, by 'getting the basics right', transformed a poor and polyglot city into a successful modern nation. Singapore's growth story has been miraculous, attracting the attention of scholars, politicians and policy-makers from around the world eager to decipher its success formula. A key component in this was the government's post-independence industrialisation plan – the government assumed a more proactive entrepreneurial role by establishing state enterprises in key sectors such as manufacturing, finance, trading, transportation, shipbuilding and services (Ramirez and Tan 2003). This was done while simultaneously offering incentives to foreign MNCs to set up operations and regional headquarters in Singapore. The government saw this two-pronged strategy as a way to provide the necessary lift for Singapore's economy to take off (Feng et al. 2004).

External trade played an important role in Singapore's emergence as a developed economy. Foreign direct investment (FDI) has contributed to Singapore's economy over the years. The World Bank also ranks Singapore as the world's easiest place to do business (World Bank 2010). Furthermore, Singapore is also fast emerging as an optimal destination for the centralisation of services or 'shared services' (SEDB 2009). Figure 1.1 refers to the trade performance of Singapore in real terms.

Figure 1.1 Trade performances in real terms

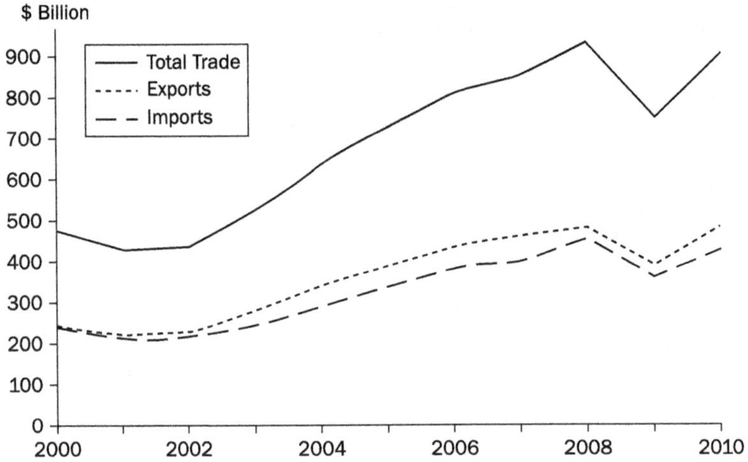

$ Billion

Prior to 2003, trade data excludes Singapore's trade with Indonesia.

Source: Statistics Singapore website

Singapore is now a highly successful and developed economy with high per capita gross domestic product (GDP). Figure 1.2 depicts the real economic growth of the country. The economy depends heavily on exports, particularly in consumer electronics, IT products, pharmaceuticals and a growing financial services sector. The main sectors and industries are: electronics, chemicals, financial services, oil drilling equipment, petroleum refining, rubber processing and product, processed food and beverages, ship repairs, offshore platform construction and entrepot trade. It had exports of US$273.4 billion (2009) within Asia to: Hong Kong (11.57 per cent of the total); Malaysia (11.47 per cent); China (9.76 per cent); Indonesia (9.67 per cent); South Korea (4.65 per cent); and Japan (4.56 per cent).

Singapore's real GDP growth rate averaged 6.8 per cent between 2004 and 2008, but contracted by 2.1 per cent in 2009 as a result of the post-2008 global financial crisis. Figure 1.3 illustrates the share of GDP by industry.

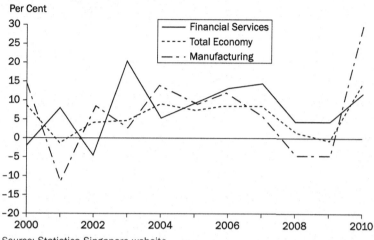

Figure 1.2 Real economic growth

Per Cent

Legend:
- Financial Services
- Total Economy
- Manufacturing

Source: Statistics Singapore website

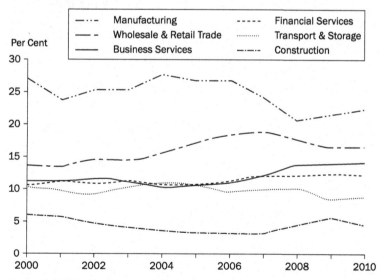

Figure 1.3 Share of GDP by industry

Per Cent

Legend:
- Manufacturing
- Wholesale & Retail Trade
- Business Services
- Financial Services
- Transport & Storage
- Construction

Source: Statistics Singapore website

In 2009, GDP at purchasing power parity (PPP) was US$251.3 billion and GDP per capita (PPP) was US$53,900 (CIA World Factbook 2010). It is instructive to look at Singapore in comparison to some other Asian countries in such areas and some pertinent labour market dimensions. These can be seen in Table 1.1.

From this we can see that Singapore is very small in population and labour force size, and dwarfed by its neighbours in many respects. Singapore also has a relatively low percentage of people under 15 (only Japan's level is lower) and a high median age (again only higher than Japan's figure), although its population growth rate is roughly in the middle (better than Japan, South Korea, Thailand and China but worse than Malaysia, Indonesia and Vietnam) of the Asian countries in our comparison. Such demographic trends have worrying long-term implications for the labour force and strains in the labour market. This is in terms of older workers leaving the labour market and fewer new workers entering the labour market and no option to draw on surplus agricultural workers as a 'reserve army of labour' – unlike many of Singapore's Asian neighbours. Of course other alternatives, such as extending working life and immigration, could ameliorate this strain to some extent. Indeed, our Centre for Seniors case study (in a later chapter) provides an example of some possibilities in this area.

The post-2008 global financial crisis had significant impacts on Singapore as a whole, particulary affecting its labour market. By 2009 there were 3.03 million people in the labour force (76.2 per cent in services and 23.8 per cent in industry), comprising 1.99 million (65.5 per cent) residents and 1.04 million (34.5 per cent) non-residents (MOM 2009: 2). Reflecting the weak job market, the proportion of residents aged 25 to 64 in employment fell for the first time in 6 years, down to 75.8 per cent in June 2009, from a peak of 77 per cent in 2008, as more people became unemployed (MOM 2009: 12).

Table 1.1 Singapore and Asian economies compared in key labour market dimensions

Country/ Competitor type	Population (million)	Of which <15 (%)	Median age (years)	Growth rate (%)	Labour force (million)	In agriculture (%)
Singapore *Developed*	**4.7**	14	40	0.863	**3**	0
Japan	**127**	13	44	-0.191	**66**	5
South Korea *Developing*	**49**	17	37	0.266	**24**	7
Thailand	**66**	21	33	0.626	**38**	43
Malaysia *Emerging*	**26**	31	25	1.723	**11**	13
China	**1,339**	20	34	0.655	**813**	40
Indonesia	**240**	28	27	1.136	**113**	42
Vietnam	**86**	25	27	1.137	**48**	56

Source: Estimates from CIA The World Factbook (2010)

With people as Singapore's only natural resource, it is obvious how critical it is to optimise these human resources (HR) and its human capital for its success. To cope with the labour market challenges and to offset the recession, the government subsidised wages, lowered corporate taxes, guaranteed bank loans and spent more on infrastructure as part of a S$20.5 billion (US$13.6 billion) stimulus package (Datamonitor 2009).

Interestingly, the economy has proved to be somewhat resilient and has withstood the challenges of the global economic crisis. Thus, after a contraction of minus 6.8 per cent in the fourth quarter of 2009 (Gov Monitor 2010), Singapore claimed the title of fastest-growing economy in the world in 2010, with GDP growth of 17.9 per cent in the first half of that year (Ramesh 2010). Indeed, the annual GDP growth rate of 14.7 per cent in 2010 was a record (even surpassing 1970's dazzling 13.8 per cent) driven by a surge in the fourth quarter in manufacturing (of 28.2 per cent), while services (accounting for 65 per cent of GDP) also grew (by 8.8 per cent) (BBC News 2011).

Over the longer-term the government hopes to establish a new growth path that focuses on raising productivity. As part of this, the government has attracted major investments in pharmaceuticals and medical technology products and will continue efforts to establish Singapore as South East Asia's financial and hi-tech hub. Figure 1.4 notes Singapore's direct investment abroad as well as foreign direct investment in Singapore.

Thus, education and human capital development are critical to Singapore. English is the main language of instruction in Singapore, which spends 3.2 per cent of GDP on education (CIA World Factbook 2010). We can see the route map of Singapore's education in the Appendix (Ministry of Education 2010). This also provides details on the stages

Figure 1.4   Investment

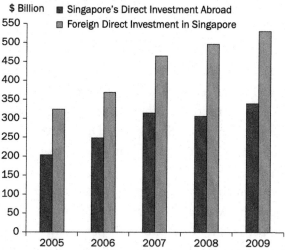

Source: Statistics Singapore website

in education. Primary education is six years, covering English, mother tongue and maths as well as science, social studies, civics and moral education, music, arts and crafts, health education and physical education. Secondary education is four years in special/express, or normal (academic), or normal (technical) courses. Tertiary education is composed of junior colleges/centralised institute (for the academically-inclined pre-university two and three year course), polytechnics (more applied); institute of technical education; arts institutions, Singapore Institute of Technology and four publicly funded universities (National University of Singapore, Nanyang Technological University, Singapore Management University, Singapore University of Technology and Design) and continuing education (SIM University). These indigenous universities are supplemented by a plethora of foreign universities with campuses and delivery arrangements in Singapore.

Cultural

The cultural and social landscape of Singapore is multi-ethnic and multi-religious, with its people living in relative harmony. Singapore's ethnic composition is as follows: 76.8 per cent Singaporean; Malay 13.9 per cent; Indian 7.9 per cent; other 1.4 per cent (CIA World Factbook 2010), Caucasians and Eurasians (plus other mixed groups) and Asians of different origins (Singapore Department of Statistics 2010). Some 42 per cent of Singapore's populace are foreign nationals (UN 2009).

In terms of religions/beliefs, Singapore (2000 census) is: Buddhist 42.5 per cent, Muslim 14.9 per cent, Taoist 8.5 per cent, Hindu 4 per cent, Catholic 4.8 per cent, other Christian 9.8 per cent, other 0.7 per cent, none 14.8 per cent (CIA World Factbook, 2010). Buddhism is the dominant religion, with all three major traditions (Theravada, Mahayana, Vajrayana) present, although most are Chinese of the Mahayana tradition. However, Thailand's Theravada tradition has seen growing popularity and Tibetan Buddhism is also making a slow inroad into the country in recent years.

In terms of languages, Singapore has speakers of: Mandarin, spoken by 35 per cent; English 23 per cent; Malay 14.1 per cent; Hokkien 11.4 per cent; Cantonese 5.7 per cent; Teochow 4.9 per cent; Tamil 3.2 per cent; Chinese dialects 1.8 per cent; other 0.9 per cent (CIA World Factbook 2010). The government recognises four languages (English, Malay, Mandarin and Tamil) with English the dominant language, which became widespread after 1965 when it was implemented as a first language medium in the education system, and in 1987 it was declared the official first language of the education system.

Following our context-setting for Singapore in terms of the historical, political socio-economic background, we next provide details of how our research was undertaken. This is in terms of the types of fieldwork and how it was conducted.

The research and methods

This book is based on research concerning the experiences of managers and their organisations operating in Singapore. This was conducted by the SHRI Research Centre, Singapore in 2009. The work covers the views, key measures, risk management strategies and innovative solutions these organisations had, and wished to have, in order to remain sustainable. The organisations covered a range of sectors, sizes and types (see Table 1.2), with SMEs, voluntary welfare organisations (VWOs) and large local organisations as well as long established MNCs with origins in Asia (India, Japan, Malaysia, Singapore), Europe (France, Sweden, Switzerland, UK) and the Americas (US, Mexico).

The fieldwork for our research took six months. We used a case study method. Rather than using samples and following a rigid protocol to examine a limited number of variables, case studies were developed that involved in-depth, longitudinal examination of a single instance or event. Together these cases provide a detailed and nuanced way of

Table 1.2   Number of organisations by type

Type of organisations	Number
VWOs	4
Large local	7
SME	15
MNCs	24
Total	50

Source: SHRI (2009)

looking at events, collecting data, analysing information and reporting results. As a consequence of this, the researcher gains a sharper understanding of what has happened and what might become important for future research (Bent 2006).

Some 489 organisations were 'purposely' chosen as they were active SHRI members, organisations and participants and represented the HR profession. From this group some 70 organisations (due to resource constraints) were 'randomly' picked. Some 50 organisations expressed their willingness to take part in the project and research, out of which 27 wished to contribute their ideas anonymously and the remaining 23 were happy to be identified, although within this group some individuals did not want to be quoted directly, such as those at Fuji Xerox and iqDynamics. These organisations all operated in Singapore and were invited to participate through e-mail which was later followed up by telephone calls.

Therefore, the methodology applied was 'random purposeful sampling' where the cases were chosen at random from the sampling frame of a purposefully selected sample. Overall, the objective of the study was to understand the phenomenon of business sustainability in our time frame of the then current post-2008 global economic crisis situation in Singapore. Though not being technically 'representative' of the country, the cases to an extent did portray the situation.

In short, the diverse sectors and size of organisations in our research provided a wide array of means and measures resorted to in order to try to achieve business sustainability in a globalised environment. Further details of the numbers of different types of organisations and their sectoral coverage and spread can be seen in Table 1.3.

Data from the organisations were collected through a suitable mix of methods. We detail these next. First, focus groups were used. The focus group method is a form of group interview in which there are several participants (in addition

Table 1.3 Number of organisations by sector

Industry sector	Number
Chemicals	2
Document Processing	2
Electrical and Electronics	2
Energy	2
Event Management	2
Financial Service	2
Food and Beverage	2
Healthcare	2
Hi-Tech	3
Hotels and Leisure	3
Information Technology	5
Marine (logistics, oil and gas)	4
Media and Communications	3
Medical Technology	3
Recruitment and Consultancy	2
Retail	3
Security Services	2
Social and Community	2
Training and Consultancy	4
Total	50

Source: SHRI (2009)

to the moderator/facilitator). There is an emphasis on a particular, fairly tightly defined topic and the focus is upon interaction within the group and the joint construction of meaning. Some five (due to resource constraints) focus group discussions of three hours each were conducted at the SHRI office. The group size of between nine and eleven people was considered ideal because that is traditionally considered a normal size. The composition of a focus group was based on the homogeneity or similarity of the group members (SMEs,

Table 1.4	Focus groups by number and type of organisations	

Focus group	Participant number	Organisational type
1	10	SMEs/VWOs(19)
2	9	
3	9	Large Locals (7 + 2 MNCs)
4	11	MNCs
5	11	MNCs
Total 5	Total 50	

Source: SHRI (2009)

VWOs, large local firms and MNCs). Table 1.4 provides further details of the composition of these groups.

Second, interviews were conducted. Interviews are particularly useful for getting to the story and the details and nuances behind a participant's experiences. The interviewer can pursue in-depth information around the topic. Interviews may be useful as a follow-up to certain respondents to questionnaires, for example, to further investigate their responses (McNamara 1999). Some 25 interviews of 30 minutes each were conducted at the SHRI office with representatives chosen randomly from the participating organisations, except for two (Discovery and Nuvista), which were conducted over the telephone.

Third, secondary sources were used. This included organisations' websites, annual reports, newsletters, as well as published news in the media, books, journals, and so on.

For analytical purposes we also developed a typology of 'types' of firms. Greiner (1972) proposes a model that explains growth in organisations as a predetermined series of evolutionary and revolutionary phases. Thus, in order to grow, organisations pass through a series of identifiable phases or stages of development and crisis, exhibiting a similar pattern of change. Five phases are proposed, with growth through:

1. creativity

2. direction

3. delegation

4. coordination

5. collaboration.

Each growth stage encompassed an evolutionary phase (prolonged periods of growth where no major upheaval occured in organisational practice) and a revolutionary phase (periods of substantial turmoil in organisational life). The evolutionary phases are hypothesised to be about four to eight years in length, while the revolutionary phases are characterised as the crisis phases. At the end of each one of the stages an organisational crisis will occur and the business's ability to handle these crises will determine its future.

An analogy can be made between such models and processes of growth in an organisation and the number of years of its existence. Initially, these terms were developed to subtly observe how these organisations behaved on the basis of their age; whether the ideologies and experiences of newly formed organisations differed from that of their more experienced counterparts. On the basis of this and their age, our case organisations were put into the following classifications by type as: 'Newbie' (less than 5 years old), 'Young' (6–20 years old), 'Experienced' (21–50 years old), 'Mature' (51–100 years old) and 'Veteran' (over 100 years old). A summary of our organisations willing to be identified (23) using this classification, and adding in other key aspects, is listed in Table 1.5.

We researched different sized organisations, both small and large. SMEs in Singapore, as elsewhere around the globe, are seen to be shock absorbers, innovators and

Table 1.5 Summary of case organisations willing to be identified

Name	Industry	Origin	Products/Services	Founded	Staff	Type
SMEs and VWOs						
Asia Polyurethane Manufacturing Pte Ltd	Chemical	Singapore	Blends and supplies customer designed polyurethane resins and manufactures polyurethane blended components for wide range of industries	1985	<50	Experienced
Atlas Sounds & Vision Pte Ltd	Retail	Singapore	Quality sound and vision lifestyle solutions	1962	65	Experienced
Caelan & Sage Pte Ltd	Training and consulting	Singapore	Training and consultancy services	2007	<50	Newbie
Centre for Seniors	Social and community	Singapore	Promotes total well-being of seniors, particularly vocational, financial and psycho-social well-being	2006	<50	Newbie
Egyii	Training and consulting	Singapore	Helps financial organisations get better results through their people's relationship skills	2009	<50	Newbie

Company	Industry	Location	Description	Year	Employees	Category
iqDynamics Pte Ltd	Information technology	Singapore	Provides business application solutions and consultancy for human capital management school and campus management, club memberships, ERP, CRM software	1994	50	Experienced
Jason Electronics Pte Ltd	Electronics	Singapore	Specialises in design, supply, installation and service of maritime electronics solutions for shipping, off/onshore and oil and gas industries	1976	160	Experienced
KH Security Agency Pte Ltd	Security services	Singapore	Private security company	1998	169	Young
MHC Asia Group Pte Ltd	Healthcare	Singapore	Web-based information systems for historical data of workforce health and disease patterns. Third party administration and consultancy services related to employees' health and design and customized health care plans	1996	<50	Young
NuVista Technologies Pte Ltd	Information technology	Singapore	IT outsourcing services for engineering, manufacturing and banking sectors	2002	<50	Young

(Continued)

Table 1.5 Summary of case organisations willing to be identified (Continued)

Name	Industry	Origin	Products/Services	Founded	Staff	Type
SG Net Fashion Development Pte Ltd	Retail	Taiwan	Fashion outfits	1991	<50	Experienced
TME Systems Pte Ltd	High tech	Singapore	Distribution of world-class and cutting-edge technology products and solutions in testing and measurement and embedded computing and industrial automation solutions	1986	<50	Experienced
Large Local Organisations						
Heatec Jietong Pte Ltd	Marine, oil and gas	Singapore	Expert services in heat transfer and piping systems	1990	650	Young
KTL Offshore Pte Ltd	Marine, oil and gas	Singapore	Supply rigging equipment and related services to offshore oil and gas, marine and construction industries	1973	NA	Veteran
MNCs						
AP Communications Pte Ltd	Event management	Singapore	Integrated marketing solutions, ranging from strategic planning and creative services to audience marketing and event management	1997	>100	Young

Autodesk Inc.	Information technology	USA	Develops 2D and 3D design software for use in architecture, engineering and building construction, manufacturing and media and entertainment	1982	6,600 worldwide	Experienced
Discovery Networks Asia Pacific	Media and communication	USA	International television businesses in media industry, delivering quality content designed to inform, entertain and inspire	1994	NA	Young
Europhia LLP	Training and consultancy	Singapore	Recruitment and executive search, consultancy and training services specialised in logistics and supply chain industry	2006	<50	Young
Fuji Xerox Singapore Pte Ltd	Document services and business consulting services	Japan	Suite of solutions ranging from document management, content management to knowledge management	1965	NA	Experienced
Givaudan Singapore Pte Ltd	Fragrance and flavour industry	Switzerland	Creator of tastes and scents	1895	8,772 worldwide	Veteran

(Continued)

Table 1.5 Summary of case organisations willing to be identified (Continued)

Name	Industry	Origin	Products/Services	Founded	Staff	Type
Polaris Software Lab Ltd	Information technology	India	Financial technology, with comprehensive portfolio of products, services and consulting	1993	9,200	Young
Teradata Corporation	Information technology	USA	Hardware and software, develops and sells a relational database management system with the same name. Specialises in data warehousing and analytic applications	1979	6,000 worldwide	Experienced
Yum! Brands Inc.	Food and beverage	USA	Fast food restaurants	1997	900,000 worldwide (including company owned and franchise operations)	Young

Source: SHRI (2009)

contributors to the country's economic growth. SMEs play a significant role in terms of employment generation and creating a productive consumer base. To some extent local SMEs help reduce dependency on organisations outside national geographical borders, thereby reducing impacts due to external volatility.

In general, often an SME is classified as such by criteria as the number of employees and the amount of capital or turnover. However, the level of these often varies across countries. Here we give some pertinent examples. In the US the definition of a small business is set by the Small Business Administration (SBA) Size Standards Office government department. The SBA uses the term 'size standards' to indicate the largest a concern can be in order to be still considered a small business (and, therefore, able to benefit from targeted funding). The concern cannot be dominant in its field on a national basis and it must also be independently owned and operated. There are size standards for each individual North American Industry Classification System (NAICS) coded industry. This variation is intended to better reflect the important industry differences. The most common size standards are (SBA 2010):

- 500 employees for most manufacturing and mining industries
- 100 employees for wholesale trade industries
- US$7 million of annual receipts for most retail and service industries
- US$33.5 million of annual receipts for most general and heavy construction industries
- US$14 million of receipts for all special trade contractors
- US$0.75 million of receipts for most agricultural industries.

The UK's Department for Business, Innovation and Skills (BIS) defines SMEs as organisations having fewer than 250 employees with either an annual turnover not exceeding €50 million or a balance sheet totalling €43 million, and not part of a larger enterprise that would fail these tests (BIS 2010). An SME is defined by the European Union as an independent company with fewer than 250 employees and either an annual turnover not exceeding €40 million or a balance sheet not exceeding €27 million (European Commission 2010).

Across Asia several definitions of SMEs are used. India's Rural Planning and Credit Department of the Reserve Bank of India (RBI) defines an SME as a small scale industrial unit, an undertaking in which investment in plant and machinery, does not exceed Rs.1 (approximately US$217,000), except in respect of certain specified items in hosiery, hand tools, drugs and pharmaceuticals, stationery items and sports goods, where this investment limit is Rs.5 crore (often abbreviated cr, this is a unit in the Indian numbering system equal to ten million or 100 lakh and it is widely used in the Indian business context). Units with investment in plant and machinery in excess of the SSI limit and up to Rs.10 crore may be treated as 'medium enterprises' (RBI 2010).

In China the definition of SME varies across industries (Li and Rowley 2005). However, usually an organisation with less than 100 employees is considered an SME.

In Japan an organisation with less than 300 employees, or holding assets worth ¥10 million (approximately US$119,660) or less is usually considered an SME. There are further restrictions in wholesaling (less than 50 employees, ¥30 million assets or less) and retailing (less than 50 employees, ¥10 million assets) in defining SMEs (APEC 2010).

The Standards, Productivity and Innovation Board (SPRING) Singapore, a statutory board under the Ministry of Trade and Industry defines SMEs as those with S$15 million (US$9.8 million) or less in fixed asset investment and, for non-manufacturing enterprises, 200 or fewer employees. In 2010 some 99 per cent of all enterprises in Singapore were SMEs employing six out of every ten workers and contributing almost half of the national GDP (SPRING Singapore 2009).

We also researched large firms. Though there is not a clear, universal definition of large local organisations, for the purpose of our study we defined them as those which were incorporated in Singapore and had greater fixed asset investment and number of employees than SMEs.

In addition, we also researched MNCs. According to the International Labour Organisation (ILO), MNCs include enterprises, whether in public, mixed or private ownership, which own or control production, distribution, services or other facilities outside the country in which they are based (ILO n.d.). The Organisation for Economic Co-operation and Development (OECD) defines MNCs as those companies (home) or other entities whose ownership is private, state or mixed, established in different countries (hosts) and so linked that one or more of them may be able to exercise a significant influence over the activities of others and, in particular, to share knowledge and resources with the others. The degrees of autonomy of each entity in relation to the others vary widely from one MNC to another, depending on the nature of the links between such entities and the fields of activity concerned (ILO n.d.). The first modern MNC was the Dutch East India Company, established in 1602.

Singapore has been able to attract MNCs to invest and establish a wide range of business activities. Many of these organisations have even set up their regional headquarters in Singapore. According to a Ministry of Trade and Industry Singapore estimate, there are more than 6,000 MNCs in

Singapore (MTIS n.d.). The recent report released by the Economic Strategies Committee (ESC) notes the local conducive environment allowing Singapore to become a globally leading 'living lab' for businesses to conceptualise, co-create, test bed and commercialise future-ready solutions for global and Asian markets, making Singapore an ideal 'living lab' grounded on the ability to pilot with speed, scale and integrity, with a compact urban environment for controlled experimentation, testing and leading adoption (ESC 2010).

Structure of the book

Our book has five further chapters. Chapter 2 briefly outlines the meaning, metrics and measurement of business sustainability, Triple Bottom Lines (TBLs) and introduces the concept of businesses life and linking and reaffirming an organisation's existence with philosophies. Chapter 3 presents a mix of recent cases of how SMEs, VWOs, large local organisations and MNCs perceive business sustainability. Chapter 4 covers organisational views on business sustainability in terms of: core values, key challenges, reasons for unsustainability, measures taken, risk management strategies, and future challenges. Chapter 5 covers some innovative practices adopted by various organisations, addresses how to raise awareness about business sustainability and introduces an integrated model of it. Finally, Chapter 6 reaffirms our stance and concludes that business sustainability is actually about more than just organisations lasting a long time. Rather, it is a conscious and integrated effort balancing the social, economic and environmental factors.

Conclusion

The impact of the post-2008 global financial crisis and its commensurate economic turmoil for organisations was the background for this research and book. We were particularly interested in business sustainability. Businesses were concerned about how they could continue and survive in the post-crisis environment and what their future concerns should be. As our research and organisational cases and examples show, they did so in different ways.

This book provides an Asian perspective on business sustainability and is about understanding how recent developments and future actions in one part of the world will have a global impact. Our book looks into the topic of business sustainability from a broad and integrated approach to business, encapsulating people, prosperity and planet, our 3Ps. It acknowledges the contributions, challenges and potential of not only big businesses, but also smaller ones. It also analyses the benefits organisations can attain with better governance, social and environmental practices.

This chapter has introduced the context of this book and its basis to readers and set the stage for the next chapter. This introduces the theme of the book and helps readers to discover better the essence of business sustainability.

2

The depths and heights of business sustainability

Abstract: This chapter introduces the essence of business sustainability from a broad and integrated approach to business, encapsulating people, prosperity and planet – our 3Ps. It also introduces the concept of a business' 'life' with the objective to reaffirm an organisation's linkages with the philosophies of life. It highlights the fact that successful and sustainable organisations have formed their basis of sustenance through 'karma', consequently creating and strengthening the basis of 'immortalising' their businesses.

Key words: 3Ps, business longevity, business sustainability, globalisation, immortalising of business, karma, people, planet, prosperity, sustainability continuum, triple bottom line (TBL).

Introduction

New business infrastructure and competitive human capital (Rowley and Redding 2011) within a dynamic labour market are some of the factors that lead organisations to make radical shifts and redefine their business strategies and enhance people management practices (Rowley and Harry 2011). Addressing these developments efficiently means organisations have to strike a balance with their limited resources and constraints as they work towards business excellence and sustainability (SHRI 2009).

What is business sustainability all about? How can businesses remain sustainable? What are some of the impacts of globalisation on the sustainability of businesses? Is it feasible for businesses to continue to prosper for long periods of time? Can businesses draw lessons from ancient civilizations? Is there a way to measure and predict the business sustainability of organisations? This chapter examines these questions and issues and helps suggest some possible answers.

The structure of the rest of this chapter is as follows. We have five further sections covering: the context of globalisation; organisational life cycles and factors affecting business sustainability; bottom lines in business sustainability; a business sustainability continuum; metrics and measures of business sustainability. These sections are followed by a conclusion.

Business sustainability and globalisation

The word sustainability is derived from the Latin word *sustinere* (*tenere*, to hold). Sustainability is seen as by some as: 'at the intersection of environmental, economic, and societal stewardship' (ASU n.d). The concept of sustainability was defined by the Brundtland Commission of the United Nations as: 'development which meets the needs of the present without compromising the ability of future generations to meet their own needs' (Brundtland 1987: 8). This is a widely quoted definition of sustainability and sustainable development.

Globalisation has a long history, both in its meanings, practices and debates. It often describes international economic competition and its impact on 'connectedness', specifically, the increasing trans-boundary flows of goods and services, including not only materials, but also information, environmental pollution and people.

The meaning and newness of globalisation is contested (see Rowley and Benson 2000). There are a variety of ways of viewing globalisation. It can be taken as involving both macro and micro aspects. On one hand there is a process of integration of national economies, while on the other hand there are significant changes in markets (product and financial), assisted by their common liberalisation and deregulation.

As with many concepts, there is rarely a universally accepted and commonly-used definition of globalisation and trying to more tightly pin-down its 'meaning' is problematic (Amin and Thrift 1996). For some it is a 'process of extending interdependent cross-border linkages in production and exchange' (Kozul-Wright 1995: 139). For others it is the integration of national economies in terms of trade and investment, with erosion of barriers (including to FDI and 'outsourcing') increasing capital mobility (Harcourt 2000). Globalisation can indicate the internationalisation of production, trade and markets and the integration of domestic economies into global economies (Burgess 2000). For others (Zhu and Fahey 2000) globalisation reflects the three integration processes of:

1. financial and currency markets;
2. production, trade and capital formation across national boundaries;
3. functions of global governance partially regulating national economic, social and environmental policies.

Also, globalisation is associated with growing internationalisation of the processes of production and finance with the decline of states and the importance of national politico-economic entities (Hadiz 2000). Importantly, we need to distinguish between financial and manufacturing globalisation because of the latter's lower mobility, longer-term focus and more direct impact on employment (Bhopal and Todd 2000).

As a simple, broad, encompassing working definition we would suggest globalisation here be seen as an erosion of the political, social and economic boundaries of nation states and markets. This does not attach reasons for globalisation, but does point to a number of key issues, such as the influence of MNCs (via FDI etc.); limitations on national laws to protect labour; a power shift towards capital; difficulties for labour organisations and trade unions in attempting to influence the process; and the level at which action needs to be taken. In short, while globalisation is a process driven by technology, sustainability seems very clearly to reflect a perception of our role in the history of nature (Runge 1997).

The above definitions and approaches make one thing very clear – that sustainability and globalisation are not contemporary scenarios, but rather have been there all through civilisations, including as far back as Ancient Rome. The main difference to this today is technological advancement and the current context, leading to increases in the frequency of such happenings and making the overall phenomenon more complex. Therefore, the issue of sustainability of businesses under globalisation actually involves another look into the fundamentals in the current context.

Life expectancies of organisations

Business sustainability may be described as cohesively managing and integrating the financial, social and environmental facets of the business. It is about creating long-term stakeholder value. Yet, how long is long? Some authors (such as de Geus 2002) talk about a company (or business) as a 'living entity' that has its own unique characteristics. Thus, it may be inferred that business sustainability is equivalent to the life expectancy of an organisation. There is a long stream of research applying naturalist 'life cycle' concepts, with birth, growth, maturity and decline (and death), to different aspects of business, from products to companies and industries (Vernon 1966, 1979; Hirsch 1967; see reviews in Rowley 1994, 1996, 1998, 2000). These terms remain in common parlance.

What then is the average life expectancy of an organisation? The Shell study described in de Geus (2002) calculated the average life-expectancy of a large MNC to be 40–50 years. However, this study only included companies that had already survived their first 10 years, commonly a period of high corporate mortality. A study by Stratix Consulting Group calculated the average life expectancy of firms in Japan and much of Europe, regardless of size, at 12.5 years (de Rooji 1996). Another study indicated the average life span of companies to be 12–15 years (Hewitt 2004). It is worrying to look at the above figures and grasp that the average life of a company is so short.

On the other hand, some organisations are still around after very long periods of time. For example, Beretta, the Italian firearms maker, is 500 years old and Giraudan the Swiss perfumery was established in 1895 (see our later case study). A 2009 study by Tokyo Shoko Research Ltd (in Breitbart 2009) notes that among nearly 2 million (1,975,620) firms in Japan 21,066 firms were founded more than a century ago and eight firms were founded more than 1,000 years ago, with Osaka-based construction company Kongo Gumi topping the list with 1,431 years of history. There are also other examples, such as South Korea, and elsewhere in the world (see Table 2.1).

Table 2.1 International examples of long-existing companies

Top 7 oldest firms in South Korea		Year founded	Sector
1	Doosan	1896	Food/Beverage
2	Dong Wha Pharmaceutical	1897	Chemical
3	Kyungbang	1919	Textile
4	Kangwon Express	1921	Transportation
5	Samyang Corporation	1924	Food/Beverage
6	Korea Express	1930	Transportation
7	Sungchang Enterprise	1931	Lumber

Oldest firms in major countries		Year founded	Sector
Japan	Kongo-gumi	578	Construction
Germany	Schloss Johannisberg	768	Wine
France	Eyguebelle	1239	Wine
China	Bejing Glazed Products	1267	Chinaware
Russia	Tysmenytsia Fur Company	1638	Textile
US	Zildjian Cymbal	1623	Instrument
Canada	Molson	1786	Beer

Source: Adapted from Kim (2008)

There were 3,146 firms founded over 200 years ago in Japan, 837 in Germany, 222 in the Netherlands and 196 in France (Kim 2008). Japan's construction company Kongo-gumi was established in 578. Regarding the reason for the longevity of Japanese firms, it has been suggested that they focused on their core businesses by accumulating and developing unique skills and know-how, based management on the trust of stakeholders, and established a professional CEO system and conservative management (Kim 2008). Korea's oldest firms date from the late 1890s, Doosan in food and beverages and Dong Wha Pharmaceuticals (Kim 2008). Cases like these prompt the view that a 'natural' average lifespan of an organisation can be much higher than the more recent averages may, at first sight, imply.

Does that mean there is an urgent need look again into the entire concept of sustainability? Why be concerned about business sustainability at all? It is because, as de Geus (2003: 3) states: 'the damage that results from the early demise of otherwise successful companies is not merely a shuffle in the Fortune 500 list, work lives, communities, and economies are all affected, even devastated, by premature corporate deaths.' Is there, then, a way for organisations to increase the length of their lives? We look at this next.

Business longevity

The Bhagavad Gita, the sacred Hindu scripture enumerates that the soul of no living entity dies. The following is noted in chapter 2, verses 22 and 23 respectively.

vāsānsijīrNāniyathāvihāyā
navānigrihNātinaro.aparāNi
tathāśarīrāNivihāya
jīrNānyanyānisanyātinavānidehī
(Vasansijirnaniyathavihayanavanigrihnatinaroaparnai,
thatasariranivihayajirnanyanyanisanyatinavanidehi,
Bhagwad Gita, chapter 2, verse 22).

Meaning – *Just as a man giving up old worn out garments accepts other new apparel, in the same way the embodied soul giving up old and worn out bodies verily accepts new bodies.*

nainaṃchindantiśastrāṇi
nainaṃdahatipāvakaḥ

nacainaṃkledayantyāpo
naśoṣayatimārutaḥ
(NainamChindantiSastrani, nainamdahatipavaka,
nachainamkledayantiapo, na so sayatimahruta,
Bhagwad Gita, chapter 2, verse 23).

Meaning – *Weapons cannot harm the soul, fire cannot burn the soul, water cannot wet and air cannot dry up the soul. The soul is eternal.*

Drawing lessons from the above and considering the fact that organisations are living entities, it may be inferred that business sustainability has two different phases. These are as follows.

1. When the business has its physical existence – this is driven by karma ('action' or 'deed'). This karmic phase is responsible for shaping the future.

2. When the business leaves a legacy behind – based on the previous karmic phase. This stage is the phase beyond physical existence of the business or post-karmic phase. The product, artefact, creation and thoughts are implanted in future generations.

The karmic and post-karmic phases of business sustainability are further explained through the following examples. In the late 1800s Marconi developed the radiotelegraph system, which served as the foundation for the establishment of numerous affiliated companies worldwide (Roy 2008). In 1902 a transmission from the Marconi station in Nova Scotia, Canada became the first radio message to cross the Atlantic from North America (Eaton and Haas 1995). Another example concerns three of Thomas Edison's inventions – the phonograph, a practical incandescent light and electric system and a moving picture camera – which helped found giant industries that changed the life and leisure of the world. For instance, by 1890 Edison had brought together several of his business interests under one corporation to form Edison General Electric. At about the same time the Thomson-Houston Company, under the leadership of Charles A. Coffin, gained access to a number of key patents through the acquisition of a number of competitors. Subsequently, General Electric was formed by the 1892 merger of Edison General Electric and Thomson-Houston Company (GE n.d.). The organisation sustained for over a century, carrying forward the legacy and also became one of the world's largest companies (Forbes 2009). These examples are able to reinforce the fact that every organisation, like humans, has a choice and the potential to live through the karmic phase, creating products or services that will form the basis of the sustainability of the organisation, even after its mere physical existence. The sustainability of business, thus, can be in its 'immortalisation', or longevity consciously created through karma.

Factors affecting the sustainability of business

Now that the karmic and post-karmic phases of an organisation have been outlined, there is a need to understand the factors that may affect the sustainability of a business in the karmic phase. As mentioned previously, the foundations of the post-karmic phase will be developed when the organisation has its physical existence. Broadly speaking, there are two factors that affect business sustainability when an organisation has its physical existence, or is in the karmic phase. These are as follows:

1. 'Regular Maintenance' – this helps the organisation to run on a day-to-day basis and acquire strength for any contingencies that may crop up in the future.

2. 'Withstanding Contingencies' – this is an organisation's ability to withstand any unforeseen challenges that may hinder the business operations and remain invincible.

As Tracy (2008: 138) notes: 'Perhaps the greatest enemy of personal success is explained by the Law of Least Resistance. Just as water flows downhill, most people continually seek the fastest and easiest way to get what they want, with very little thought or concern for the long-term consequences of their behaviour. This natural tendency of people to take the easy way explains most underachievement and failure in adult life.' Does this mean that the uncertainties of the future are created due to the selfishness of a few people governed by the law of least resistance? Assuming the present is the testing ground of future consequences, are we able to then control the present and determine the future to make it sustainable? One interesting insight into human tendency is put metaphorically: 'in Mayan mythology, the Universe was destroyed four times, and every time the Mayans learned a sad lesson and vowed to be better protected but it was always for the previous menace ... 2,000 years later we are still looking backward for signs of the upcoming menace but that is only if we can decide what the upcoming menace is' (Lynch and Rothchild 2000: 86–7).

Yet, of course, predicting the future has limitations; it is probably best to make a business more fundamentally strong so that it can withstand adversities and contingencies rather than triggering distress calls (such as 'SOS' or 'Save Our Souls'). On the contrary, revisiting fundamentals may provide options as to whether to continue to succeed or fail and go under. This in turn requires answering questions about what the bottom line in business sustainability is.

Bottom lines in business sustainability

Any uncertainty a business faces will heighten the stance of any organisation to be vigilant and creative to stay relevant and sustainable. It is a holistic picture of how businesses should strive to achieve the TBL of balancing the overlapping and inter-acting economic, environmental and social factors of the organisation, given the human capital at hand. This mix can be seen diagrammatically in Figure 2.1.

Figure 2.1 The triple bottom line of business sustainability

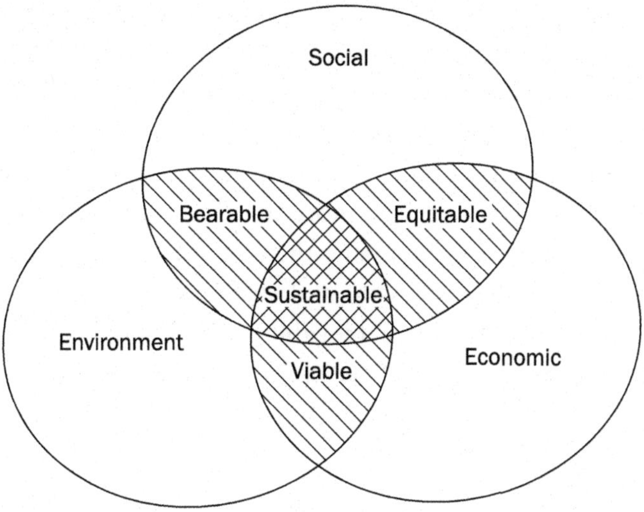

Source: Adapted from IUCN (1994)

Sustainable development is often presented as an attempt to reconcile three types of constraints: economic, social and environmental. This takes into account the interactions between them and how they contribute towards development that is: equitable (sharing of economic resources among the citizenry), viable (compliance with environmental needs), and bearable (socially and humanly acceptable) (Biaye

2010). Thus, the three objectives of the TBL – economic well-being, environmental health and social equity – requires viability from the economic and environmental point of view; equity from the economic and social point of view and being bearable from the environmental and social point of view. These are represented in our diagram (see Figure 2.1) with 'sustainability' being the 'sweet spot' where the three constraints mentioned above are balanced.

The 1990s witnessed the emergence of 'sustainability' as a corporate strategy. Early on the Business Council for Sustainable Development, a group of executives from major MNCs, such as Dow Chemical, DuPont and Royal Dutch/ Shell, expressed concern at the emerging environmental crisis and appealed for a change among MNCs – for them to break with conventional values and ways of doing business.

Businesses, as a result of their evolution and experiences in adverse economic conditions, began to realise that business sustainability was actually more about ensuring long-term business success encompassing the 3Ps of people, prosperity and planet. To be successful and sustainable, organisations must also focus on the achievable overall progress, which includes benefiting people, promoting prosperity and protecting the planet through innovative ideas (Mukherjee Saha 2009). The 3Ps have in turn been encapsulated in the concept of the TBL. This phrase was coined by Elkington (1998), later expanded and articulated in his book *Cannibals with Forks: the Triple Bottom Line of 21st Century Business* (1998). The TBL captures an expanded spectrum of values and criteria for measuring organisational (and societal) success: economic, environmental and social (see Figure 2.1).

The concept of the TBL requires that an organisation's responsibility is to stakeholders rather than simply to shareholders. In this case, stakeholder refers to anyone who is influenced, either directly or indirectly, by the actions of the organisation. At a high level, TBL sustainability is a values- and ethics-laden vision of the organisation, it is a concept that explicitly acknowledges the importance of relationships between an organisation's economic performance and its performance in social and environmental terms.

There are many tools available to assess business sustainability practices and policies adopted by various organisations. Rather than giving an 'either/or' answer of 'yes' or 'no', a more graduated picture is needed. Thus, these tools can reaffirm an organisation's position along a business sustainability continuum, as explained next.

Sustainability continuum

The Oxford dictionary defines a 'continuum' as continuous sequences in which adjacent elements are not perceptibly different from each other, but the extremes are quite distinct. A sustainability continuum covers, thus, the various ranges and levels of sustainability practices and policies adopted by organisations.

Furthermore, a Global Sustainability Continuum (GSC) has been developed as a tool to assist organisations gain a more objective, external perspective of their sustainability performance as communicated through their publicly available material (RMIT 2009). A GSC assessment places an organisation in one of five sustainability positions ranging across:

1. not sustainability aware;

2. compliance driven;

3. cost/reputation driven;

4. competitive advantage driven; to

5. sustainability leader.

After assessing the level of sustainability, an organisation may be curious to affirm the financial value and worthiness of the sustainability initiatives that they have undertaken. In order to do this, it is useful to have some understanding of various metrics and measurements relating to the dynamics of business sustainability. The next section briefly explains these.

Measures of business sustainability

There are many metrics that organisations, managers and researchers can use to conceptualise business sustainability and assign some financial values to business sustainability investments. For example, some recent research suggests that there are a total of 39 unique measures of sustainability to examine the relationship between business sustainability and financial performance (RNBS 2008).

Thus, sustainability metrics are incredibly varied, reflecting the diverse nature of sustainability itself. Many studies use a single sustainability measure, most commonly something like the following: pollution control or output; environmental, health and safety investments; third party audits or awards; the KLD (KLD Research & Analytics, Inc.) index; and *Fortune* magazine rankings.

Research Network for Business Sustainability (RNBS 2008) also suggests that there are three categories of metrics that are relevant to sustainability. These are as follows.

1. Financial: these are the end-state metrics with which the market evaluates performance. For example, return on equity from a profitable sustainable product line.

2. Operational: these are the metrics related to sustainability activities and their direct bottom-line impacts. For example, tonnes of waste recycled into manufacturing inputs and subsequent decreased raw material costs.

3. Strategic: these are the metrics that reflect an organisation's improved position strategically to create value and manage risk. For example, satisfaction rates with a community engagement programme that helped fast-track the regulatory approval process to build a new plant.

Conclusion

In this chapter we briefly outlined globalisation, defined business sustainability and introduced the concept of businesses 'life' with the objective to re-affirm an organisation's linkages with the philosophies of life. The core intention of every organisation is succinctly explained by de Geus (2002: 11) as follows: 'Like all organisms, the living company exists primarily for its own survival and improvement to fulfill its potential and to become as great as it can be . . . You exist to survive and thrive; working at your job is a means to that end. Returning investment to shareholders and serving customers are a means to a similar end for IBM, Royal Dutch/Shell, Exxon, Procter & Gamble, and every other company.' In other words, all these successful and sustainable organisations have formed their basis of sustenance through 'karma', consequently creating and strengthening the basis of 'immortalising' their businesses.

Organisations often develop expectations to be just economically prosperous. Paradoxically, such short-termism and skewed views often lead to organisational mortality. Organisations do not survive as long as they could. By viewing the whole picture and adhering to TBLs, organisations can remain more sustainable and survive longer. Therefore, businesses and organisations may succeed or fail due to their own behaviour and actions. These ideas are outlined and discussed further in our next chapters.

3

Business sustainability in practice: case studies and examples

Abstract: Any uncertainty an organisation faces will make it more vigilant and creative in ensuring business viability. During such periods, productivity in general, and innovation in particular, will be the order of the day. Together with brand reputation, real leaders focus on the need for creativity and reflection on the purpose, process and people of the enterprise to stay relevant and sustainable. This chapter presents 17 contemporary, short case studies and vignettes focusing on different organisational types: SMEs and VWOs (9), large local organisations (2), MNCs (6), with reference to what their managers think about business sustainability and the ways they dealt with the recent economic downturn.

Key words: case study, small and medium enterprises (SMEs), large local organisation, voluntary welfare organisations (VWOs), multinational corporations (MNCs).

Introduction

The global credit crunch had spread and developed to become a full-blown financial and economic crisis by 2008.

It affected many economies around the world. This triggered a general slowdown in economic activity and business cycle contraction. Many businesses, irrespective of their nature, size and geography, faced external as well as internal challenges.

Singapore was similarly impacted. Singapore is strategically located at the southernmost tip of the Asian continent and at the crossroads of the world's global trading centres like India and China. Being at the financial hot spot of Asia, organisations in Singapore passed through a similar roller-coaster phase as many elsewhere. There were increasing concerns about how organisations could remain sustainable in such an environment and global crisis. While the Singapore economy has bounced back, it still remains important to look at the situation, not least for indications of what might have contributed to this.

We bring this area of business sustainability to life by allowing organisatons to 'speak' on this subject, via short case studies and vignettes. This chapter has the following structure. It is divided into three broad sub-sections each focusing on different organisational types: SMEs and VWOs (9 in number), large local organisations (2) and MNCs (6), with reference to what their managers think about business sustainability and the ways they dealt with the economic downturn.

SMEs and VWOs

The first group of organisations we present are SMEs and VWOs. These nine cases cover a range of sectors, from retailing to training and consultancy, IT, security services to electronics and chemicals and healthcare, as well as responses to the post-2008 economic crisis.

Case Study 3.1: Asia Polyurethane Manufacturing Pte Ltd (APU): innovating through the downturn

Established in 1985, APU is an SME with less than 50 employees and a chemical manufacturer specialising in the blending and supply of customer designed polyurethane (an organic polymer) resins and manufacture of polyurethane blended components for a wide range of industries, such as domestic appliances, automotive components, petrochemical insulation projects, furniture industries, general construction and many others. Following the direction of the Montreal protocol, APU has been supplying cyclopentane systems since 1997. In 2004 APU received its first 'Enterprise 50' award and in the following year it was certified under the Singapore Quality Class, a testament to the commitment of the entire company to service and quality. APU was recently ranked in the SME 500 list of Singapore companies. Priority to customers, passion for excellence, people enhancement, partnership focus and involvement in community activity, are the core values of APU.

The post-2008 economic downturn was challenging for APU. There was lower demand for products, uncertainty over the prospects for recovery of the market, issues about ensuring sufficient cash flow and problems in HRM areas, such as managing employees, expectations, retention and attracting talent. APU realised that if there was a decrease in demand for the items that they had been producing, then there was a need to revisit the product line and it was better to go back to basics. For example, APU faced decreased demands for refrigerants due to high costs, so it embarked on an alternative, thermo ware, which was more cost effective and helped to better address the demands of the mass market. Demand for this product increased remarkably, which according to the CEO, gave rise to a 'happy problem'.

According to the CEO, Mr Erman Tan, business sustainability boils down to sufficiency of cash flow to operate an organisation. It is about remaining profitable and maintaining a buffer to be able to sustain at least for the next six to twelve months. As he put it: 'Irrespective of good or bad times, organisations need to emphasise on cost-management, retain current staff and strive towards attracting new talents. Economic downturn brings along challenges as well as opportunities. This is the period to source (raw materials) aggressively, develop quality yet cost competitive products, sell more and reap the profits back to buy more.' Mr Tan believes that the greatest challenges facing APU will be to write off old stock, proper planning with respect to expansion and diversification and implementing a just-in-time strategy. '(Now) it is the fast fish that will eat slow fish. Act fast!' he concludes.

Sources: Interview with Mr Erman Tan (2009); focus group discussion (2009); APU (2009); UNEP (2004).

Case Study 3.2: Atlas Sound & Vision Pte Ltd: RIPE in action

Established in 1962, Atlas is a Singaporean SME with 65 employees and a premier provider of quality sound and vision lifestyle solutions. The founder of the company, the late Mr A. B. Tien, branched out from the record library business into offering advice for sound systems and eventually to providing premium equipment for quality sound. During the late 1960s Atlas secured the Bose distributorship and imported Bose 901 speakers. Since then Atlas has built a strong reputation as a leading premium audio visual retailer and distributor and is the sole distributor for the brands like Bose, Loewe, Kimberkable and Noo'ance. It is a niche player in the audio visual industry, active in both B2B and B2C markets in Singapore, Malaysia and Australia.

Following the founder's death in 2003, his son Michael took over the business as CEO. In 2006, Atlas HiFi was re-branded as Atlas Sound & Vision to sharpen the company's competitive edge in providing quality sound and vision by creating extraordinary experiences for customers. It also unveiled a new generation of stores under the 'Atlas Experience' concept. The core values of Atlas rest on the four pillars of: Respect, Integrity, Passion and Excellence (RIPE). As stated by the CEO: 'Atlas had undergone many ups and downs. It has learnt lessons from the previous downturns. There are two kinds of mistakes business fall prey to a) commission – unknowingly committing a mistake and b) omission – consciously ignoring certain actions that affect business outcome. It is during the good times that businesses usually make the worst decisions. Business sustainability to us is thus constantly reviewing processes to protect the company from committing such mistakes and differentiating one's approaches from other market players. A successful business needs to offer more than a quality product or service a better customer experience.'

Over the past 20 years Atlas set the target of 20 per cent growth year on year and a doubling of turnover every five years. It was able to ride through the 1997 Asian financial crisis and the downturn in 2005. For many years Atlas re-invested 100 per cent of profits back into the company. Today the company has a capital reserve that is equal to two years of operational expenses. Atlas has been monitoring external market conditions and was prepared for the post-2008 crisis even before it happened. Atlas has a no retrenchment or pay cut policy. The challenges were to keep this promise when sales were affected due to the downturn, and how to maintain growth.

Atlas has a 3R risk management strategy: **R**etain (employees and customers), **R**edevelop (employees' skills) and **R**einforce (the brand). It is through these strategies that it nurtures relationships both with employees as well as customers. Average employee turnover is much lower than the industry average. Each year Atlas sponsors 10 per cent of its employees to pursue higher education. It is interesting to note that even though there is no bond or clause on returning to the company, such employees stay. It seems it is all about trust between employer and employee.

Atlas has a reputation for retaining their customers (up to 70 per cent). To regularly maintain these connections, each year Atlas identifies the 100 top customers and sends them a bottle of wine on a special occasion to show the company's appreciation of the trust such customers have regarding Atlas. When traced back it was found that at least 10 per cent of these customers returned to purchase more products from Atlas stores.

For their good efforts in establishing their brands, in 2007 Atlas was conferred the Singapore Prestige Brand Award (SPBA), jointly given by the Association of Small & Medium Enterprises and *Lianhe Zaobao*, a Chinese newspaper. The SPBA recognises and honours Singaporean organisations that have developed and managed their brands effectively through various branding initiatives.

The focus for Atlas is not only on making profits, but also on giving something back to society, its CSR. Atlas' innovative initiative, 'In Harmony with Education', is particularly noteworthy in this regard. This is an inter-disciplinary children's music programme to teach basic mathematics and science using music. Atlas has also pledged to give 10 per cent of annual profits to bring the programme to Singapore schools for free. A full time Atlas member of staff is engaged to run the programme. As part of its CSR Atlas adopted Assisi Hospice and has dedicated 25th September as its CSR Day. As Mr Tien, CEO explained: 'Look at the good times and be prepared for the bad times.

Atlas believes in team work and synergy which is achieved by helping the last person cross the finishing Line. This is how a business can sustain!'

Sources: Interview with Mr Michael Tien (2009); focus group discussion (2009); ASME (2009).

Case Study 3.3: Centre for Seniors (CFS): the mantra of staying relevant

As we noted in an earlier chapter, Singapore is facing labour market and demographic challenges. Singapore is one of the most rapidly ageing nations in the world. In order to become a leading organisation for seniors by promoting their total well-being, the CFS was established in 2006, with Mr Lim Boon Heng, Minister, Prime Minister's Office and Minister in charge of ageing issues, as convenor. The CFS' less than 50 staff are committed to promoting the total well-being of seniors, particularly their vocational, financial and psycho-social well-being. The CFC's three goals are to: (1) enhance the employability of mature employees through on-going training; (2) facilitate, promote and enable mature workers to remain in active employment for as long as possible; (3) equip HR personnel, managers, supervisors and union leaders with a deeper understanding of the ageing process and issues so that they will be able to manage and optimise the abilities of older employees more effectively.

In 2007 the CFS started running its first Seniors Employability Programme (SEP). SEP is the umbrella grouping of employment and employability courses for seniors and managers of seniors. The CFS added public education programmes to educate the public, including seniors, on the myths and facts of ageing, as well as to offer strategies and tips to age optimally. Indeed one such programme to encourage older employees to continue working beyond retirement age involves: **Re**-employment: **E**quipping **A**nd **D**eveloping **Y**ourself (READY)™.

During the uncertain economic conditions of the post-2008 crisis, financial viability remained one of the greatest challenges for the CFS, along with its constant endeavour to remain relevant to its clients. Being flexible and adaptable towards meeting customer needs, keeping the costs of operations down, product differentiation and keeping products and services affordable, are the four key measures that CFS focuses on.

CFS is a member of the National Council of Social Service. As a non-profit VWO, CFS depends largely on the support of well-wishers, members of the public and corporations to fund its programmes and services. Thus, 'If a product/ service are a necessity or "must-have", the demand will still be there. The challenge emerges when consumers perceive the product/service as "good to have". For an organisation like ours business sustainability is about financial viability', notes Ms Helen Ko, Executive Director, CFS.

Sources: Interview with Ms Helen Ko (2009); focus group discussion (2009); CFS (2009).

Case Study 3.4: Egyii: establishing a business foothold

Incorporated in 2009 in Singapore, Egyii is a learning and development consultancy of less than 50 staff. It helps financial organisations gain better results through their peoples' relationship skills. Egyii derives its name from Borneo's Kapuas mud snake (Enhydris Gyii), which can change its colour spontaneously, symbolising adaptability.

Financial organisations faced many challenges post-2008 and one of the biggest was enabling their people to perform at their optimum level. Thus, the organisation employed a hard, results-oriented approach to peak performance and soft skills. For Egyii, business sustainability refers to survival. Thus: 'Sustainability is a broad concept that goes beyond mere growth. To sustain is to maintain a presence in the market. Innovation and creativity plays a major role in making an organisation sustainable. Innovation should not be solely concerned with products. Instead, innovation should be about getting every employee to be innovative and proactive, and not wait for their bosses to find solutions to problems' stated Mr Trip Allen, Director, Egyii.

As client organisation's dilemmas tend to be more financial, rather than people-focused, these impact on the business of Egyii. For example, client budget freezes for employee training and development in turn affected Egyii's cash flow. Egyii is, however, very cost-conscious, using new media platforms like social networks, blogs and word-of-mouth, etc., to promote itself. It also focuses on niche areas to stay competitive.

Being small, Egyii members keep each other motivated. They have learnt how to manage their responses to events, especially negative ones like bad sales meetings. They choose to see setbacks as opportunities. Egyii focuses on cost-management and identifying niches in order to establish a business foothold.

Sources: Interactions with Mr James Irvine and Mr Trip Allen, Directors, Egyii, during focus group discussion (2009) and subsequent e-mail correspondence.

Case Study 3.5: iqDynamics Pte Ltd: mitigating risk

Incorporated in 1994, iqDynamics is a 50 employee IT company. It offers and deploys affordable enterprise solutions such as HR, talent, student and club and resort management. It also offers white papers, information brochures, the latest HR news, software development and outsourcing advice. The company provides one-stop integrated software solutions to businesses across Asia, serving over 300 customers with offices in Singapore, Malaysia, Indonesia and India, as well as partner alliances in China, Vietnam and Sri Lanka.

The company has a vision to be the market leader for software solutions in the mid-market such as HR, education and hospitality segments. It clinches projects from many clients and sectors, including MNCs in manufacturing, distribution and services sectors, local large and medium-size companies, the government, universities, international schools, premier golf clubs in Singapore and the region, to name just a few. The quality work and service delivery helped the company secure third place for 'Best Outsourcing Vendor' in Human Resources Magazine, Singapore in 2006.

The iqDynamics philosophy is based on four principles: (1) awareness of change and its impact; (2) responsibility to people they are working with; (3) commitment to getting the job done; (4) action in transforming ideas into deliverables. The company believes business sustainability is about maintaining a constant flow of revenue and having a strong customer base which makes it easier to survive crises. Re-deployment of resources, managing costs and focusing on innovative new products and services were some of the key challenges iqDynamics faced during the post-2008 economic downturn. The company constantly endeavoured to foray into newer markets and diversify products and services whenever feasible to manage their business risks. Furthermore, the company established more open communications with their employees to further boost the morale of their employees and reinforce the fact that the company management was in support of its employees in both good and bad times. This was a proactive approach of the management to have a happy and engaged workforce. This resulted in lower employee turnover and increased overall customer service levels.

Sources: Interactions with Mr Lim Say Ping, founder and Director during focus group discussion (2009) and subsequent e-mail correspondence.

Case Study 3.6: Jason Electronics Pte Ltd: embracing long-termism

Established in 1976, long-termism is the mantra of sustainability for this 160 staff SME. Headquartered in Singapore, having overseas representative offices in South-East, South and East Asia, Jason specialises in the design, supply, installation and service of maritime electronics solutions for shipping, offshore/onshore and the oil and gas industries. It was conceived as a sole proprietor company to service the marine electronics industry as Jason Marine and two years from its inception was incorporated into a private limited company. Jason Electronics is the wholly owned subsidiary of Jason Marine. Its customers are from the international shipping market – deep sea ships, coastal and inland shipping, dredging, government and military, offshore (oil and gas), mega yacht shipyards and fisheries. The organisation is driven by the Jason 3Cs: **Character:** responsibility, integrity, honesty, reliability, hardworking, discipline; **Competence:** innovative, experience, continuous improvement, committed to quality; **Commitment:** passionate, perseverance. The company was awarded the 'Singapore SME 500' and 'Enterprise 50 Awards' in 2004.

Jason was among the first Singapore companies to be certified with the Technical Reference (TR) 19:2005 standard in Business Continuity Management (BCM) which has helped them in withstanding the post-2008 crisis situation. The TR19:2005 is a BCM standard – published by SPRING Singapore in 2005, providing Singapore-based enterprises with a framework to respond to, and recover from, potential disruptions. It covers disciplines such as risk management, disaster recovery and crisis management. It is a preventive measure meant to help organisations stay vigilant and resilient; thereby enabling them to run their business uninterrupted even in the event of a crisis.

With the post-2008 economic downturn, Jason put more emphasis on inventory management and control to reduce waste and increase operational efficiency. This was achieved by helping employees identify their training needs in order to better manage inventory and streamline operations accordingly. It also focused on employee engagement and increased the frequency of internal communications between management and employees. Jason conducted dialogue sessions with employees and promoted open communications which helped in keeping employees motivated as the employees felt more involved by partnering the company management in the progress of the organisation.

With the aspiration to be an employer of choice, Jason is a firm believer in work–life balance. For example, it has been steadfastly running various programmes for employees to enhance their overall welfare. Such commitment to employee well-being was recognised when it received the 'Family Friendly Employer Award' in 2004 and 'Singapore Health Award' (Bronze and Silver) consecutively for 2004, 2005 and 2006. Jason's two in-house committees, Recreation Club and Workplace Health Club, take charge of helping employees maintain a better work-life balance. These committees regularly arrange activities, such as year-end parties, health talks, healthy sandwich competitions, yoga lessons, nautical runs and bowling competitions.

Furthermore, Jason Marine, the parent company, has an in-house CSR committee, JE@Heart, formed in 1996 in the belief that strong family values are the crucial foundation of society. JE@Heart activities are based on three core beliefs: (1) promoting strong family values; (2) volunteering in community projects; (3) supporting youth development. The organisation seeks to act as the bridge for employees to engage in community service.

Jason recognised that this approach is not just about monetary contributions, but the opportunity for employees to share their passion with the people around them. Jason is one of the inaugural signatories to the Singapore Compact, which is a participant of the United Nations' Global Compact. As was stated: 'Business Sustainability is about making decisions on a long-term philosophy even at the expense of short-term financial goals. (Over the years) the company has learned to adapt to changes in market conditions and environment and is proud to be serving the highly sophisticated marine electronics industry in the Asian region. The company's philosophy has always been to excel in all her pursuits whether in innovation, leadership or customer service but never at the expense of human dignity, honesty and integrity. Jason is also a firm that practices social responsibility in society', Mr Ooi Chee Kong, Chief HR Officer.

Sources: Interactions with Mr Ooi Chee Kong during focus group discussion (2009) and subsequent e-mail correspondence; Jason (2009); SPRING Singapore (2008).

Case Study 3.7: KH Security Agency Pte Ltd: building relationships

KH is a private security company founded in 1998. KH's vision is to have a strong capacity to work and develop prudent and responsible procurement relationships for buyers, police and private individuals – gearing towards total security and professionalism. In one of the comprehensive and stringent grading exercises by the Security Industry Regulatory Department, which is part of Singapore police force, KH was graded 'A' (Excellent).

KH is a unionised company under the Union of Security Employees with 169 staff. It is one of the signatories of the tripartite guidelines for fair employment practices in Singapore. The company firmly believes in recruiting the right talent based on fair employment practices, establishing long term relationships with clients and rendering services efficiently and effectively. KH took the opportunity stemming from the post-2008 economic downturn and emphasised building relationships with their client companies.

KH also decided not to cut wages or to make employees redundant, no matter how bad the situation became. Such initiatives helped KH strengthen its brand image for both internal, as well as external, stakeholders. KH focuses on the needs of each individual employee. It takes advantage of its small size to achieve this through a more informal and personalised structure. It also provides working opportunities to mature workers. KH supports employees by providing them with varying choices to cater to differing family and personal needs. One example is KH providing a two-day working week for a 67-year old employee, Mr Ho, who wanted to spend more time with his grandchildren but at the same time to continue working.

In order to embed the good practices internally, the company has a mentor-buddy system. Under this initiative a senior staff member is allocated to each new joiner for a one month period to help them through the initial phases of employment and familiarise themselves with corporate culture. The mentor is usually of a similar family background and same gender.

During the post-2008 economic downturn KH also obtained available government funding to maintain their staff costs. One of the other key measures KH took during the downturn was training employees to keep them abreast of the ever-changing environment. All employees completed the Security Workforce Skills Qualifications provided by the Singapore Workforce Development Agency (the statutory board under the Ministry of Manpower, Singapore) for the private security industry. KT's constant endeavours and people-focused practices helped the organisation not only stay afloat, but also win many accolades like:

(a) 'May Day Award' 2007, conferred by the Singapore National Trades Union Congress to organisations and individuals in recognition of their efforts of significant and sustained contributions to the labour movement through the promotion of good industrial relations, strong support for training initiatives and helping workers improve their welfare.

(b) 'The Singapore HR Awards' 2009, organised yearly by SHRI, celebrating leading organisations and HR practitioners in their drive for impactful human capital strategies in the leading HR practice category Health/ Employee Wellness and Fair Employment Practices respectively, to name a few.

Thus, to sum up, for Mr Gary Harris, Senior Business Development Manager: 'Business sustainability is about branding the products and services of the company to reach closer to the stakeholders.'

Sources: Interactions with Mr Gary Harris during focus group discussion (2009) and subsequent e-mail correspondence; SWDA (2009); NTUC (2010).

Case Study 3.8: Nuvista Technologies Pte Ltd: expanding into newer markets

NuVista is a 35-employee, ISO 9001:2000 certified engineering and IT outsourcing SME established in Singapore in 2002. It provides services in the engineering, manufacturing and banking sectors. The core value of the company rests on four pillars: (1) understanding customers' requirements and market needs; (2) understanding staff capabilities and implementing training to ensure the fullest realisation of their potential; (3) implementing cost-effective and efficient operations; (4) setting effective quality objectives to continually improve the quality management system.

In 2006 NuVista was awarded a contract by Honeywell to provide commissioning and site engineers for projects based in Qatar and South Korea. A year later Nuvista Technologies Pte Ltd incorporated Nuvista Staffing Solutions Pte Ltd (providing executive search in engineering and IT). In 2008 Nuvista Technologies opened offices in Pune to cater to their Middle East and Indian clients. In 2009 an agreement with engineering companies in the Middle East to provide recruitment and procurement services was signed. NuVista was included as a representative for International Enterprise's (IE) business mission to the Middle East to explore business opportunities. IE Singapore is an agency under the Ministry of Trade and Industry spearheading the development of Singapore's external economy.

Thus: 'The current recession has not lent a great impact on the company as we are in a niche market and the life cycle of the projects that we were into are long. We responded fast to change as per the changing external conditions and explored into newer markets. For example, NuVista is focusing on expanding its business in the Middle-East like Qatar, Abu Dhabi and Saudi Arabia. Business sustainability is about maintaining revenue by optimising cost of operation. Customer satisfaction is of topmost priority and NuVista strives towards it by providing defect-free solutions and services, on-time and every time, at an optimum price' states Mr Vijay Bareja, Director.

Sources: Interactions with Mr Vijay Brajera during focus group discussion (2009) and subsequent e-mail correspondence.

Case Study 3.9: TME System Pte Ltd: focusing on employee development

Established in Singapore in 1986 with six employees, TME has come a long way, expanding the business, albeit with still less than 50 staff, to represent more than 30 product lines and establishing a presence in Indonesia, Malaysia, Singapore and Thailand. TME is a premier high-tech solutions and services provider. Its core capabilities are in the distribution of world class and cutting edge technology products and solutions in testing and measurement and embedded computing and industrial automation solutions.

TME believes business sustainability boils down to sustainable business practices that can be applied in other areas in the organisation, such as having a business model that would sustain itself in its profitability as well as to grow and expand in the long run. To do this, there is a strong need for corporate governance and direction driven from the top and implemented at the operations level. For example, during the post-2008 economic downturn, TME saw a drastic reduction in demand for its goods and services. TME realised the need to be more strategic in the deployment of resources and to stay even more competitive. Management played a critical role in leading staff to a common vision and roadmap to recovery for when the economy picked up. In other words, the management of the organisation shared their vision with their employees and also established a two-way communication system where employees also expressed their expectations from the workplace. This ensured that the goals of management and employees were well aligned. Cost-management measures were put in place to ensure the company came out of the recession faster and it is highly effective in its business execution. These include more cautious approaches to business travel during recession, seeking alternatives to travel like web conferences to fulfil business objectives, and so on.

The greatest challenge for TME is developing a business model that has a vision and roadmap for growth and expansion. This entails three aspects: (1) a compelling mission and vision; (2) a robust and attractive set of corporate values that would attract the right talent; (3) firm and decisive leadership and management to execute the business plan to fulfil its mission and vision.

With over 20 years of experience in the supply chain of these core markets, TME has accumulated immense expertise in identifying technology trends and market needs and meeting these needs. The company's continual success is attributed to the strong commitment to the following triple sales value proposition: (1) partnership – partnering with customers to determine their needs and working with vendors to exceed the expectations of customers; (2) differentiation – differentiating from the competition to deliver the best quality products and services to customers; (3) innovation – providing innovative technology solutions that are effective for customers' deployment. In 2008, TME was awarded 'Singapore SME 500 Company' status by DP Information Group.

Importantly, TME also believes HR can play a strategic role in its sustainability by constantly facilitating communications between top management and employees and helping them meet their mutual workplace expectations.

HR also plays a pivotal role in managing relationships with stakeholders, adding value to the productivity and profitability of the organisation. HR is not seen as a sunk cost. Thus: 'For an SME like ours to grow, we are always trying to retain talents by giving them ample opportunities to develop their skill sets as well as add value to their personal and professional lives. We also see it as one of the ways to develop notable employees as part of succession planning' argues Mr Ronald Soo, Managing Director, TME.

Sources: Interactions with Ms Lisa Ong, Group HR/Admin Manager during focus group discussion (2009); interview with Mr Mark Woo, General Manager, TME Systems and subsequent e-mail correspondence with Mr Ronald Soo; TME (2009).

Large local organisations

The post-2008 global financial crisis and its economic impacts also influenced large organisations, the second group we covered. The examples follow of two large local organisations from the marine, oil and gas and support sector, and their responses and views on business sustainability.

Case Study 3.10: Heatec Jietong Pte Ltd: managing risk by training locals

Heatec is the Singapore-based leading large organisation in the marine, oil and gas industry, providing expert services in the field of heat transfer and piping systems. It employs 650 people. Its history goes back to 1990 when JieTong

Engineering was formed with 14 staff to provide piping services to local shipyards, mainly the Keppel Shipyard. In 1994 Heatec Asia Pacific Pte Ltd was founded with 10 employees catering for the heat exchanger needs of the marine market in Singapore. In 2001 Heatec Asia Pacific and JieTong Engineering merged to form Heatec JieTong Pte Ltd. In the subsequent years Heatec extended its market outside Singapore. A service facility, Heatec Shanghai Co Ltd, opened in China, the start of Heatec's pursuit of a global presence.

In the context of Heatec, a labour-intensive company where 90 per cent of workers are foreigners, business sustainability requires a constant supply of HR, managing of the culturally diverse group of workers and maintaining social cohesion within the workplace. For Heatec, business sustainability is the ability of the organisation to survive both in good and bad times. The post-2008 economic downturn posed a set of challenges, such as searching for a large and diversified client base, managing high fixed costs and regulatory obligations. For instance, Heatec usually needed employees who were skilled in a very niche area. Locally, it was difficult to acquire or develop such a HR pool within limited periods of time. So, Heatec relied on foreign workers and made efforts to retain them in good and bad times, hence it had to maintain high fixed costs. For example, in Singapore organisations employing foreign employees pay the Foreign Worker Levy (FWL), a pricing mechanism to control the number of foreign (including domestic) workers. The challenge for Heatec was to keep paying the FWL even when the business was not as good as in previous years. Indeed, Heatec felt that the levy had increased very fast in the good times, but had not been revised during the bad times. In fact, the FWL will be gradually raised and the tiers tightened over the next few years as the government moves to reduce dependence on foreign workers further.

Thus: 'The core values of Heatec Jietong are to strive to achieve and enhance customer satisfaction by on-time delivery of quality products and services through competent resources. We constantly focus on customer satisfaction, process conformity, product conformity, supplier evaluation and resource competency. Going forward, the company is devising risk management strategies focusing to search for a large and diversified client base as well as training locals with the required skill-sets to reduce dependency on foreign workers', states Ms Jacqueline Soon, HR Manager.

Sources: Interactions with Ms Jacqueline Soon during focus group discussion (2009) and subsequent e-mail correspondence; EnterpriseOne (2009).

Case Study 3.11: KTL Offshore Pte Ltd: roping in growth

KTL Offshore Pte Ltd, a subsidiary of KTL Global Ltd, is one of the leading players in the oil and gas support services sector, with offices in Singapore, Vietnam and Dubai. Once a traditional family business, KTL evolved and enhanced its expertise to serve its clients in the Asia-Pacific region in a more professional manner. KTL was listed on the Singapore Exchange Securities Trading Limited in 2007, with a turnover in 2008 of S$63 million (approximately US$49 million).

Despite stiff competition from both within Singapore and abroad, KTL was selected to supply the complete heavy lift package for the prestigious project of the decommissioning of topsides, steel support jackets and a section of the associated 12 inch gas export pipeline which lay in 150 metres of water at an offshore field 40 kilometres east of Naraha Cho, Fukushima prefecture, Japan. Weighing more than 20,000 metric tonnes, this was the largest platform to be decommissioned in Japan to date.

Indeed, KTL in 2011 will be amongst the top three suppliers in the world to the offshore oil and gas and related industries for wire rope, rigging and heavy lift products and services. This success is attained by delivering their five core principles of business philosophy: (1) implementation of market expansion and penetration strategies which are focused, pinpoint and effective; (2) providing wire rope and rigging products and services on a scale that cannot easily be matched by competitors in terms of size, quantity and availability; (3) delivering the highest quality products and services and the most reputable brand name in the industry; (4) providing a total solutions concept for the most demanding problems faced by the market, through innovation, commitment and professionalism; (5) developing personnel through investment in training to become experts in their field.

Thus: 'Business sustainability is all about the capability to survive at any time by improving the service standards and attracting more clients. One of the key challenges faced during economic downturn was to offer relevant services to the highly competitive market. We had a constant focus on sales and made all efforts reaching out to clients' states Ms Vanise Koh, HR Assistant Manager.

Source: Interactions with Ms Vanise Koh during focus group discussion (2009) and subsequent e-mail correspondence.

MNCs

The post-2008 global financial crisis and economic turmoil also impacted on MNCs, the third group of organisations that we covered. This section provides an overview of six MNCs with their origins in India, Japan, Switzerland and

USA, covering sectors ranging from documentary services to fragrance and flavouring (F&F) and food and beverages.

Case Study 3.12: Autodesk Inc.: innovating and growing

Autodesk, a US MNC, focuses on 2D and 3D design software for use in architecture, engineering and building construction, manufacturing and media and entertainment. Founded in 1982 by John Walker (a co-author of early versions of the company's flagship CAD software product, AutoCAD) and 12 others, it is the world's largest design software company, with more than 9 million users throughout the world. It is headquartered in California and has approximately 6,600 employees worldwide.

Autodesk's first notable product was AutoCAD, an application designed to run on the systems known as microcomputers at the time, including those running the 8-bit CP/M operating system and two of the new 16-bit systems, the Victor 9000 and the IBM personal computer. This CAD tool allowed users to create detailed technical drawings, and was affordable for many smaller design, engineering and architecture companies.

With the purchase of Softdesk in 1997, Autodesk started to develop specialty versions of AutoCAD targeted at broad industry segments, including architecture, civil engineering and manufacturing. Since the late 1990s the company has added a number of significant non-AutoCAD based products, including Inventor, an internally developed parametric mechanical design CAD application in 1999, Revit, a parametric building modelling application acquired in 2002, etc. In 2006, Autodesk acquired Alias. In the same year, Autodesk was named by *Fortune* magazine as one of the '100 Best Companies to Work For'. The organisation's acquisition spree continued in 2007 with Skymatter Inc, developer of Mudbox and the technology and product assets of Opticore AB, based in Gothenburg, Sweden, and California-based PlassoTech, developers of CAE applications. In 2008 Autodesk acquired Kynogon SA, the privately held maker of Kynapse artificial intelligence middleware and REALVIZ S.A., Avid's Softimage, Co. As can be seen from the above, Autodesk is forging ahead on a growth path. It was recently listed number 25 on *Fast Company*'s 'The World's 50 Most Innovative Companies'.

Autodesk's foundation rests on its core values of: respect, teamwork, flexibility and risk taking and with a vision to provide solutions that allow customers to realise their ideas. Thus: 'For businesses to be sustainable, it is important to think long-term rather than adopt short-term measures. It is probably time to go back to the basics and think of eliminating the elements in excess from the business processes so that the system can run efficiently,' says Doug Kelly, Talent Acquisition Manager, Autodesk Singapore.

During the post-2008 economic downturn the challenge that Autodesk faced was the dilemma of laying off employees as a cost-cutting initiative. The company believes that managing innovation and innovative employees is going to be the greatest challenge facing the organisation. Thus: 'As an industry leader we do not intend to simply weather this economic storm. We are taking actions to improve our cost structure and enhance our design technology, which in turn will help our customers become more efficient and provide them with a competitive advantage. As we look at our business today, we are confident that our technological leadership, brand recognition, breadth of product line, and large installed base position us well for success and the eventual recovery of the economy' states Carl Bass, Chief Executive Officer and President, Autodesk Inc.

Sources: Interactions with Mr Doug Kelly during focus group discussion (2009) and subsequent e-mail correspondence; Autodesk (2009).

Case Study 3.13: Fuji Xerox Singapore Pte Ltd: collaborate to compete

The origin of Fuji Xerox Singapore dates back to 1965 when it was still part of Rank Xerox, a joint venture (JV) between Rank Organisation and Xerox Corporation. The Singapore branch was first incorporated as Rank Xerox (Overseas) Pte Ltd, later renamed Rank Xerox (Singapore) Pte Ltd in 1985. In 1991 Rank Xerox Singapore was sold to Fuji Xerox Company Ltd of Japan, (itself a 50–50 JV company between Fuji Photo Co. Ltd and Xerox Corporation) and renamed Fuji Xerox Singapore Pte Ltd. In 2001 Xerox sold 50 per cent of its stake in Fuji Xerox to Fuji Photo Film Co. Ltd. and retained 25 per cent ownership interest. Fuji Xerox Singapore Pte Ltd is now a wholly-owned company of Fuji Xerox Asia Pacific, together with other operating companies in Australia, Indonesia, Malaysia, New Zealand, the Philippines, South Korea, Taiwan, Thailand and Vietnam.

For over 40 years Fuji Xerox Singapore has stood out as a premier document production and processing equipment leader with a significant share of the markets for advanced colour printers and multi-function document systems. From a history as a copier company, Fuji Xerox has evolved to become the leading provider of document and knowledge management solutions. Today the company provides cutting edge software, hardware, consulting and business services that effectively help businesses to capture, archive, retrieve and distribute knowledge residing in multi-faceted document forms. As the key innovator in the enterprise content management arena, Fuji Xerox provides a suite of solutions ranging from document management, content management to knowledge management. Supported by a team of consultants and solution architects, the organisation's commitment is to help businesses transform complex information and experience into knowledge with innovative solutions to enhance competitiveness, accelerate growth and increase revenue.

In recent years Fuji Xerox experienced tremendous growth and underwent a massive transformation from merely a device manufacturer to become a provider of document management solutions. Headed by President/Managing Director Bert Wong, Fuji Xerox Singapore experienced robust growth when it widened its focus from selling devices to forming long-term partnerships with companies and organisations that use its solutions and services. To better represent the new direction of its changing business, Fuji Xerox launched a new corporate logo in April 2008. This sphere-shaped symbol, called 'Sphere of Connectivity', symbolised partnerships with customers and society as well as being a global brand image. The new logo was designed with soft, curved lines to emphasise close relations and affinity with customers and society. The new logo represents innovative changes, enterprising spirit, vigor and dynamism and shows that Fuji Xerox has gone beyond just the document arena.

The company has gained market leadership in all of its main business areas, including digital devices, colour devices, solutions and services. The most notable recent achievement for Fuji Xerox Singapore has been a much coveted Singapore government award. Fuji Xerox Singapore consolidated its status as a lead partner in the One Meridian Consortium that won the US$1 billion Standard ICT Operating Environment (SOEasy) project that involves standardising the operating environment across the whole government on a similar platform. This will enable government staff to concentrate on being productive and doing what they need to do instead of handling thousands of different devices from different brands. Fuji Xerox has the ability to transform the whole government from a device-based organisation to a service-led organisation in terms of their document output through managed print services. The company hopes to use this project as a showcase for other governments around the world. The company's innovative approach to create and deliver value has paid off.

According to the company, business sustainability is about how an organisation can continue to add value to stakeholders and community in the mid- and long-term. The post-2008 economic downturn posed challenges for the company, such as maintaining a balance between business profitability and sustainability, ability to sustain customers and keeping employees motivated and engaged.

The culture of the company is based on its four core values of: (1) fighting spirit; (2) collaborate to compete; (3) innovation and learning; (4) care and concern. It believes that aligning its corporate culture with the core values have helped them create a strong sense of belonging for staff and an environment to continue to learn and innovate. It is especially important during the bad times to have strong team-bonding with a high fighting spirit, it is argued. The company has also taken the key measures of focusing on critical areas, working capital and cash flow management, customer satisfaction and employee engagement and is also focusing on business continuity plans, talent management and succession plans as risk management strategies. These, Fuji Xerox believes, will help them meet their future challenges of business transformation, the changing customer landscape and talent and succession management.

Sources: Interactions with Ms Lee Soon Kim, General Manager of Human Organisation Resource and Development, Fuji Xerox Singapore during focus group discussion (2009) and subsequent e-mail correspondence.

Case Study 3.14: Givaudan Singapore Pte Ltd: glorifying a rich heritage

This Swiss MNC was founded in 1895 when young chemist Leon Givaudan established a perfumery company in Vernier on the outskirts of Geneva, Switzerland, the headquarters of Givaudan. In 1924 the company acquired Burton T. Bush of

New Jersey. In 1948, Givaudan expanded its presence by acquiring Esrolko SA, a strategic move that opened the door to the flavour industry. In 1963 Givaudan joined Hoffmann-LaRoche as a wholly-owned subsidiary of the Swiss pharmaceutical firm. Soon after this the company opened a perfumery school which today has the distinction of training one in three of all creative perfumers in the industry. Givaudan remains one of the most respected companies in the sector and has over 8,700 employees worldwide. It was the first company to establish itself as a creator of tastes and scents. Givaudan's wide range of expertise is categorised under the four innovation pillars of: (1) Sensory Intelligence; (2) Sensory Creation; (3) Sensory Technology; (4) Sensory Science.

From the early 1980s Givaudan expanded its presence into Asian and other global markets. In the late 1980s Givaudan bought Riedel Arom, a German flavour company based in Dortmund. In 1991 Givaudan bought Fritzsche, Dodge and Olcott, a well-respected US based F&F company, whose origins dated back to the late 1700s. Then Givaudan and Roure merged to create Givaudan-Roure. The merger was completed with the acquisition of Tastemaker in 1997, making Givaudan the largest flavour company in the world. In 2000 Givaudan became an independent company, entering the SMI on the Swiss stock exchange. Givaudan acquired FIS, the flavour business of Nestlé in 2002 and IBF, a leading cheese flavour company in 2003. In 2006 Givaudan acquired the F&F business Quest International from ICI Plc.

With the vision to be the essential source of sensory innovation for its customers and driven by a passion for excellence, Givaudan has dominated the F&F industry for centuries. The four core values which have enabled the company to grow and maintain its rich heritage are: (1) passion for customers; (2) performance; (3) innovation; (4) people. These values are the keys to achieving company objectives.

Givaudan has weathered several earlier economic crises. The key challenge faced during the post-2008 economic downturn was how to save resources for the future and cut requirements while maintaining high productivity. Thus: 'To remain sustainable, businesses must acknowledge individual responsibilities towards employees; promote healthy organisational culture, focus on product development, more importantly environment friendly products consequently improving on market share. Givaudan has consistently delivered long-term sustainable growth through its focus on innovation, customers and operational excellence and that is what we believe to be the secret of business sustainability' states Mr Johnathon Ng, HR Manager.

Sources: Interactions with Mr Johnathon Ng during focus group discussion (2009) and subsequent e-mail correspondence.

Case Study 3.15: Polaris Software Lab Ltd: banking on technology

Polaris is a leading financial technology Indian MNC with a comprehensive portfolio of products, services and consulting. Incorporated in 1993, it is in the business of providing world class technology infrastructure to the banking, financial services and insurance (BFSI) industry. Polaris strives to be a leader in this financial technology infrastructure space by constantly investing in superior technology, offering better functionality and enabling efficient business processes through strong focus on building expertise in their people.

Soon after its inception Polaris developed an end-to-end retail banking solution for Citibank India, thereafter setting up operations in the US. In the late 1990s its first overseas development centre was commissioned to cater to the needs of Citibank. Later, Polaris formed a wholly-owned subsidiary in Singapore and the US. During this period its initial public offering was launched, which was over-subscribed 21 times. It was then that Polaris was rated amongst the world's best small companies by *Forbes* magazine.

In the early 2000s Polaris became the world's first CMMi level 5 company. Polaris opened a business continuity centre in Singapore and launched its subsidiary Adrenalin, which later merged with OrbiTech (a Citigroup subsidiary). Now the company has 9,200 employees spread over 23 international offices, four global near-shore development centres and seven business solution centres focusing on micro-verticals in BFSI. Polaris attributes its fast growth to its business strategy which rests on the seven strategic levers of: (1) domain knowledge; (2) technology; (3) platform; (4) methodology and tools; (5) processes; (6) reusability; (7) energy, and also the five value creation areas of: (1) cost; (2) quality; (3) reliability; (4) speed; (5) flexibility. It is these strategic levers and value creation areas that Polaris believes are the essence of business sustainability.

The Polaris culture puts a lot of emphasis on learning. The Polaris ethos is that talent must be 'Humble, Hungry and Smart'; humble in attitude, hungry to learn more and smart in their approach. Polaris has made a huge shift by propagating a culture of a 360 degree learning environment where the learning sources include teammates, peers and customers. Thus: 'Polaris foresaw early in its journey that the future was never for "generalists" or "pure cost arbitrage" business. Polaris singularly focused in the BFSI segment through products and "solutioning" approach. The people expertise is developed in Polaris' Centres of Excellence. This kind of "expertise" culture is difficult to replicate and grows significantly only when it continues to accumulate the wealth of knowledge and expertise over time. Polaris has created an atmosphere akin to a university to promote continuous learning and specialized learning to be able to understand the customer pain points and create solutions to address it, and thereby create value' says Mr Nagaraj Prasadh, Director HR.

Polaris also believes in balancing business profitability and CSR. As part of their CSR initiatives the company started the Ullas trust in 1997 to nurture dreams and encourage a 'can do' spirit among economically challenged adolescent students. Polaris associates support and manage this trust. The trust organises educative and informative sessions for the students, where volunteers from Polaris teach computer and internet basics and counsel on career prospects. The company received many awards and accolades including the 'Mother Teresa Corporate Citizen' award for the successful operation of their initiative.

The company notes that the key challenge faced during the post-2008 economic downturn was how to maintain a level of trust between employers and employees. Thus: 'At times, to survive the downturn, companies have to implement policies that may not be employee friendly. Employees may not be able to see things from an employer's point of view and may misunderstand the company's objective' argues Mr. Prasadh. Polaris strives to offer a high performance workplace to its employees. It provides opportunities and stimulus packages that can trigger learning and development to enable professional and personal growth for their employees. Thus: 'History teaches that all big institutions are a result of major changes. This is an opportunity of changing leadership at the market place. Polaris being an expertise-centric organisation will have an edge,' concludes Mr Prasadh.

Sources: Interactions with Mr Nagaraj Prasadh during focus group discussion (2009) and subsequent e-mail correspondence.

Case Study 3.16: Teradata Corporation: technology matters

Teradata Corporation is a hardware and software US MNC with 6,000 staff worldwide that develops and sells a relational database management system with the same name. It specialises in data warehousing and analytic applications. The concept of Teradata grew out of research at the California Institute of Technology and the discussions of Citibank's advanced technology group. It was incorporated in 1979.

In 1986 *Fortune* magazine named Teradata 'Product of the Year'. In 1989 Teradata Corporation partnered with NCR Corporation to build the next generation of database computers. NCR was acquired by AT&T in September 1991. In December 1991 NCR announced its acquisition of Teradata. In 1992 the company pioneered the first system over 1 terabyte (a trillion bytes) that went live at Wal-Mart. In 1996 Teradata database was named the world's largest database, with 11 terabytes (11 trillion bytes) of data. In 1998 Teradata was ported to Microsoft Windows NT. In 2000 Teradata's first enterprise class application for detailed customer profitability measurement, Value Analyzer, was launched at Royal Bank of Canada. In 2001 Teradata more than doubled the lines of code (from 1.6 to 3.8 million) and later introduced its Financial Management Solution, an analytic architecture made up of hardware, software, professional consulting and support services. In 2003 more than 120 industry leading companies migrated from Oracle to Teradata after the launch of the Oracle-to-Teradata migration programme. Teradata University Network was created to advance awareness of data warehousing in the academic community. Nearly 170 universities from 27 countries were represented in the network. In 2004 Teradata and SAP announced a technology partnership agreement to deliver analytic solutions to industries with high data volume requirements. In the same year Teradata and Siebel Systems, Inc. (now Oracle Business Intelligence) announced a strategic partnership to immediately make available integrated and optimised products. Microsoft Corporation and Teradata formed a strategic alliance in 2006. In 2007 NCR announced its intention to separate into two independent companies to create two market leading companies – NCR and Teradata, each focusing on different businesses. In the same year, Teradata launched Teradata 12, an innovative, advanced database delivering traditional data warehousing for strategic planning, along with usable intelligence to frontline operations throughout the enterprise.

In 2009, InformationWeek ranked Teradata number 22 in its annual list of the '250 Top Innovators' in implementing IT. It was also selected for the seventh consecutive time by *Intelligent Enterprise* for the magazine's 2009 Editors' choice awards 'The Dozen' – their elite list of the most influential vendors that will drive the intelligent enterprise in 2009. In 2009 Teradata was included in *Business Week's* 'InfoTech 100', the world's best-performing technology companies.

Ms Wendy Soh, HR Manager, Teradata Singapore, believes: 'For businesses to be sustainable, there should be an improvement of existing products and development of new products. Doing so will allow businesses to gain a broader market share and ensures sustainability in the long run.' Having survived previous recessions, Teradata was more prepared to deal with the post-2008 one. Having a vision for a consistent, unified representation of business operations, the organisation adopted cost management, selective knowledge management and focus on leadership development as some of their risk management strategies. However, the company recognised that there was a constant challenge to hire the best talent for key positions and training employees and developing skills essential for business success.

The company also has a strong focus on CSR. This includes the Teradata Cares Program. This encourages and supports employee engagement in building strong and vibrant communities, improving quality of life, and making a positive difference where they live and work. 'Every day the company with its 6,000 odd workforce (worldwide) pushes analytical intelligence deeper into operational execution, enhancing efficiency and transforming corporate culture reinforcing their company mantra - Teradata . . . Smarter. Faster.Wins.™'

Sources: interactions with Ms Wendy Soh during focus group discussion (2009) and subsequent e-mail correspondence.

Case Study 3.17: Yum! Brands Inc: vouching for its success formula

With a vision to become the defining global company that feeds the world, Yum Brands! the US MNC began in 1997 as Tricon Global Restaurants, Inc. It acquired Long John Silver's and A&W All American Food Restaurants in 2002. Tricon underwent a name change in 2002 to Yum! Brands, the world's biggest fast food restaurant MNC in terms of system units, with over 36,000 restaurants in over 110 countries and territories and a revenue of more than US$11 billion and 900,000 employees worldwide, including company-owned and franchise operations. The company operates or licenses world famous fast food brands such as KFC, Pizza Hut, Long John Silver's and Taco Bell.

Within just a few years of its existence in the early 2000s, Yum! climbed to 15th place in *Fortune*'s 'Top 50 Best Companies for Minorities'. It had created the first Global Customer Appreciation Day to celebrate customers and recognise restaurant leaders for providing great service. It was during this period that the company was ranked in *Fortune*'s 'Top 50 Best Employers for Women'. In 2007 the company topped *Institutional Investor* magazine's corporate rankings of America's most shareholder-friendly company and best CEO in the restaurant industry. Soon after this Yum! Brands launched a global movement to stop world hunger in support of the United Nations' World Food Programme. Some 5 million volunteer hours and US$17.5 million in overall donations were gathered. During this period, Yum! Brands China was named one of the 'Top 10 Best Employers' by China Central TV.

The company also issued its first CSR report, Serving the World, reviewing the company's global social, environmental and economic impact. As part of the company's CSR, its KFC and Taco Bell outlets operated the first 'green' restaurants. Over the years, Yum! found ways to be more 'green' when it came to energy and resource usage. It also eliminated transfat from the food sold by its fast food companies. It is these efforts that helped the company appear in the *Corporate Responsibility Officer* magazine's '100 Best Corporate Citizens' list.

Thus, Mr C.K. Mohan, Senior Director, HR, Yum! Brands, Singapore acknowledges that: 'For businesses to be sustainable, they must stay relevant to their customers, even during tough times. Tough times are not entirely bad for the company as they bring opportunities. For example, tough times are good for negotiating and expanding. In order to remain sustainable an organisation must stay relevant to its customers. Thus business sustainability is all about staying relevant.'

During the post-2008 economic downturn Yum! Brands had its own share of challenges of managing costs and finding ways to increase sales and provide value to customers. The company's major risk management strategies were: aggressive international expansion and building strong brands everywhere, but with a special focus on China. There was dramatic improvement in its US brand positions and returns.

The company continued training its employees and kept looking for opportunities to grow the business. Employees were seemingly happy since the business was doing fine and no one lost their jobs. Though the company was sailing through the period, it foresaw a few challenges ahead, such as energy usage in restaurants, waste management, packaging and sustainable building design and especially HR-related challenges, notably talent attraction, training talent across all levels and leadership development.

How does the company deal with all these challenges? Mr. Mohan reveals the secret formula as: 'Our formula for success is working. When we put people capability first, then we satisfy more customers — and profitability will follow! This is the formula of how the company wins together: they believe in All people, they are customer Maniacs, they go for breakthrough solutions; build know-how, Recognise! Recognise! and Recognise!'

Sources: Interactions with Mr C.K. Mohan during focus group discussion (2009) and subsequent e-mail correspondence.

Conclusion

The previous chapter introduced the meaning of business sustainability for us and focused on some interesting perspectives. This chapter presented a mix of local cases of how SMEs, VWOs, large local organisations and MNCs perceived business sustainability. What does this show us? The post-2008 economic downturn has been a reality check for many organisations. The cases from the diverse organisations outlined in this chapter provide examples of an array of means and measures organisations resorted to in order to remain sustainable in the post-2008 crisis environment. Organisations had varied and interesting ways of looking at the concept of business sustainability. To some organisations the post-2008 economic downturn was an opportunity to strengthen their internal processes, focus on innovation and move forward – for example APU, with its innovating alternative cost-effective solution. For other organisations the post-2008 economic crisis was an opportunity to be more innovative, such as strengthening their internal processes, focusing on employees, customers, product innovation and venturing into newer territories – for example, NuVista, with its focus on expanding its business in the Middle East like Qatar, Abu Dhabi and Saudi Arabia. For yet other organisations the post-2008 economic turmoil was a matter of more traditional actions, such as cutting costs, closing units and reducing loss on balance sheets – for example, Autodesk, which had to face the challenge of laying off employees as a cost cutting initiative.

This chapter raises further questions, such as why do some organisations seem to do better than some others? Do organisations learn any lessons and look into the possibilities of being more sustainable? What similarities and differences do these organisations have with organisations operating in other parts of the world? The next chapter elaborates further on these points.

4

The challenges and the future for business sustainability

Abstract: The post-2008 global financial crisis and consequent economic turmoil indicates that organisations will either succeed or fail partly depending on their reactions and responses. All too typically, business processes are made unnecessarily complicated and bureaucratic when the solution lies in being simpler and reducing transaction costs. This chapter examines organisational views and business sustainability in terms of: core values; key challenges; reasons for unsustainability; measures taken; risk management strategies; and future challenges.

Key words: economic crisis, global financial crisis, talent, talent management, risk management, unsustainability.

Introduction

The post-2008 global financial crisis and consequent economic turmoil indicates that organisations will either succeed or fail partly depending on their reactions and responses. All too typically, business processes are made unnecessarily complicated and bureaucratic when the solution lies in being simpler and reducing transaction costs. Strategies are often skewed towards short-term business profits, ignoring the long-term effects, which may well be deleterious. For instance, as noted by the Head-Asia Pacific (Talent Management) of an international IT company operating in Singapore, downsizing has become a more fashionable cost-cutting initiative (SHRI 2009). Interestingly, despite the short-termism of the US and UK, this knee-jerk reaction has not always been the case in parts of the West with the post-2008 economic crisis (see Rowley 2010a).

Organisations may resort to headcount cuts (and also pay package reductions). Yet, this action may then reduce an organisation's talent base. If not handled properly, which is often the case, the demoralised staff that are left behind (often with 'survivor's syndrome' as it is called) will be the next to 'jump ship' when the economic environment improves. This has echoes in a quote from a business leader, that: 'Business sustainability is about being able to continuously innovate, implement and drive the right strategy to grow and sustain one's customer base (including internal customers-employees), retain and grow leadership pool and adapting to tough changes' (SHRI 2009).

We often see uncontrollable effects and analyse them in retrospect, most often ignoring the causes, which are far more controllable if the intention is for them to be controlled. To cope with economic downturns, many organisations close down business units that they thought were not significant for their future growth. A set of questions then arise. Is this actually a necessary measure? Are there any bigger problems in the system? It may be argued that in the post-2008 crises, the 'right's rights' are often shadowed by the 'wrong's might' – that the effect of the economic crisis was shared by the people who were probably the least involved (Mukherjee Saha 2009: 8).

Paradoxically, times of crisis are probably a good time, in terms of when fundamentally strong companies emerge, survive and succeed. Successful companies have a clear sense of business direction, while their business strategies and practices adapt to a changing world. They encapsulate and portray their business sustainability strategies through their corporate value system. For example, the secret of staying ahead in the competition lies in a core culture of nurturing creativity. These ideas can be seen in the case of the Discovery Networks Asia-Pacific. We show this in the box below.

Text Box 4.1: Discovery: staying ahead of the competition

'Business sustainability is about creating shareholder value for the stakeholders by continuously innovating new products/services and going closer to the customer. It also depends upon the organisation culture. Discovery is a vibrant organisation where its culture nurtures creativity, promotes employee development and engagement, be it in good or bad times. During this phase of recession, our clients have been more cost conscious. Our challenges were to provide innovative and customised solutions to our clients while maintaining the quality of our services. Going ahead our challenge would be to continuously strive for better content to stay ahead of our competition.'

Mr Andy Teng, Manager – Human Resources, Discovery Networks Asia-Pacific.

Sources: Telephone interview with Mr Andy Teng (2009) and subsequent e-mail correspondence.

The rest of the chapter has the following structure. We have five sections that cover and detail organisational views on business sustainability in terms of the following. First, core values, followed by key challenges, reasons for unsustainability and measures taken, then organisational risk management strategies and future challenges. These are followed by a conclusion.

Core values and business sustainability

Corporate values can be defined as first-order operating philosophies or principles to be acted upon and that guide an organisation's internal conduct and its relationship with the external world (Serrat 2010). Thus, corporate values articulate what guides an organisation's behaviour and decision-making and they can boost innovation, productivity and credibility, thereby helping deliver sustainable competitive advantage. This set of perspectives follows earlier views elsewhere. For example, HRM, and especially employee resourcing of organisations, are sometimes treated in a manner that has been labelled a 'downstream' or 'third order' activity (by Purcell, see Rowley 2003), that is, an activity which follows in the wake of the business strategy and which HRM practitioners implement in a somewhat mechanical fashion. This area is also linked to ideas of HR as the only 'real' source of competitive advantage (see inter alia, Barney 1991). Underpinning such views are ideas such as that: 'People are the only element with the inherent power to generate value. All other variables offer nothing but inherent potential. By their nature, they add nothing, and they cannot add anything until some human being leverages that potential by putting it into play' (Fitz-enz 2000: xiii).

Corporate values portray corporate identities. Core values form the foundation of an organisation and determine their stability and sustainability. The significance of core values is aptly narrated by the Chair and Chief Executive Officer of

Ameritech (the parent of Bell Telephone in Illinois, Indiana, Michigan, Ohio and Wisconsin): 'When a corporation enunciates a set of standards and does not abide by them . . . when we talk one way but act another — people are torn in two directions, become cynical, and cease to take the value system seriously. This undermines the drive to corporate identity and to excellence. It is important, therefore, to encourage behavior consonant with the corporation's values — even before the realization of attitude changes, which may require more time' (Stackhouse et al. 1995: 704). Thus, it is imperative for organisations to focus on values before even trying to see the bigger picture of business sustainability.

Researchers (Donker et al. 2008) developed a 'corporate value index' (CV-Index) model based on a set of parameters. This model was applied to Canadian companies listed on the Toronto Stock Exchange. It found statistically significant evidence that corporate values in general are positively correlated with firm performance and sustainability.

Corporate values are often inscribed by organisations in brochures, websites and other branding materials. These provide a snapshot of their characteristics and indicate their focus in doing business. The range of corporate values exhibited by the organisations in this book is quite varied – from loosely defined unstructured adjectives to focused and integrated objectives. It is interesting to note that most of the organisations in this book have corporate values revolving around a few key words. These key words have been collated from each organisation's website and listed in Table 4.1.

Interestingly, repetitions of words were noticed, for example, 'customer', 'cost-management', 'hardworking', were amongst the few words used by multiple organisations as their corporate values. These key words may be indicative of the current operating philosophies of these organisations.

Table 4.1   List of key words (core values)

Action	Courage	Innovation	Professionalism
Care & concern	Customer	Integrity	Profitability
Character	Differentiation	Learning	Quality products & services
Collaborate to compete	Discipline	Market needs analysis	Reliability
Commitment	Excellence	On-time delivery	Respect
Community	Fighting Spirit	Partnership	Responsibility
Compassion	Flexibility	Passion	Risk-taking
Competence	Hardworking	People	Teamwork
Continuous improvement	Honesty	Performance	
Cost-management	Humility	Perseverance	

Source: SHRI (2009)

However, one key word, 'collaborate to compete', sounded quite distinct. As can be seen from the Table, all other key words are more straightforward, having one single objective for example 'partnership', 'teamwork', etc., but it is the key word 'collaborate to compete' which has a two-step objective – such as bringing diverse functional teams together to focus on a shared purpose (PMCCB 2010).

Key challenges faced by organisations

We asked our organisations to list key challenges faced by them during the post-2008 economic downturn. These are listed in Table 4.2.

Of the nine challenges given, the top trio was by far the most commonly enunciated. These were:

1. how to and how much to cut costs and how to handle situations that occurred due to budget freezes on the client side (given by nearly nine out of ten);

2. ensuring cash flow (over two-thirds);

3. matters related to employee engagement and continuity of trust between employer and employees (nearly two-thirds).

The fourth most frequently listed challenge was exploring, or intending to explore, newer geographical locations given market saturation (42 per cent). In the case of Singapore, market saturation has become a serious threat to the long-term survival of organisations, especially many SMEs (which are mostly owned by ethnic Chinese). This market saturation is very much a consequence of the domination of the domestic market by foreign MNCs and SOEs during the industrialisation process in Singapore (Rodan 1989; Yeung 1994).

Table 4.2　　Key challenges faced by organisations (n = 50)

Rank	Key challenge	Response (%)
1	Cost cutting/budget freeze	86
2	Ensuring cash flow	70
3	Employee engagement and continuity of trust between employers and employees	62
4	Searching for new clients/venturing to different geographical locations	42
5	Work-life integration	6
6	Evergreen industry not affected by recession	6
7	Organisation producing niche products/ services hence not affected by recession	2
8	Did not face any challenges – prepared to face to recession	2
9	Saving resources for future	2

Source: SHRI (2009)

The other five challenges listed followed well behind these four, given by very few organisations (just 2 per cent–6 per cent). For example, better work-life balance (by 6 per cent) took a back seat as both employers and employees perceived such practices to equate to a loss of productivity and to be unaffordable in a crisis situation. This development is contrary to the perception that employers, as well as employees, had in early 2008, just before the crisis hit. For example, a 2008 report noted managing work-life balance as one of the key future challenges (Boston Consultancy Group & World Federation of Personnel Management Association 2008). Another example is that only a very few organisations (just 2 per cent) mentioned that even though others in their industry faced a lot of pressure from the adverse external conditions, their niches were not affected, their top management was proactive enough to cushion their organisations from becoming affected, saving at the same small percentage, seeing resources for the future as a key challenge. Thus, there were no pay cuts, retrenchments or other cost-cutting initiatives. Interestingly, such actions in turn boosted the morale of their employees and helped the organisations retain or attain a good brand image. These aforementioned trends were quite similar across most industries and size of organisation in our sample, barring those in the healthcare and security services areas. These two fields witnessed higher demand for their products and services, so were somewhat unaffected by the post-2008 economic downturn.

Reasons for unsustainability of businesses

It is noted that: 'sustainability is currently one of the most fashionable terms used by post-Marxist Progressives. The word sustainable has been slapped onto everything from sustainable forestry to sustainable agriculture, sustainable economic growth, sustainable development, sustainable communities and sustainable energy production' (Devall 2001: 1). If sustainability is such a widely referred to and well-understood term, what could be the reasons for unsustainability? When we asked our organisations for reasons, the following five were cited: poor leadership (by a huge four-fifths), resistance to change (over two-fifths), not being a 'systems' thinker (nearly a half), ignoring risk (just over one-third) and greed (over one quarter) as shown in Table 4.3. These reasons are discussed next.

As has been noted: 'Poor leadership was on display after Hurricane Katrina and during the financial crisis. The New Orleans masses who huddled in the Superdome after Hurricane Katrina, the Enron retirees who lost their life savings and the laid-off workers buried under the economic ruin of financial companies all live with a simple truth. Just as spectacularly as great leadership can spark success, failed leadership can bring down cities, businesses, and economies' (Lytle 2009: 26). The vast majority, four-fifths, of organisations believed that the rise and fall of any organisation

| | Table 4.3 | Reasons why organisations become unsustainable (n = 50) |

Rank	Key reasons	Responses (%)
1	Poor leadership (including bad governance, lack of vision, bad decisions/inability to make decisions, poor planning, etc.)	80
2	Resistance to change	68
3	Not being a 'systems' thinker	46
4	Ignoring risk	34
5	Greed	28

Source: SHRI (2009)

had a direct correlation with leadership ability, and particularly attributes related to institutionalising good governance, vision, decision-making ability and planning.

Research indicates that organisations are undergoing major change approximately once every three years, whilst smaller changes occur almost continually (CIPD 2005). There are no signs that this pace of change will slow down. In this context, managers have to be able to introduce and manage change to ensure the organisational objectives of change are met and they have to ensure that they gain the commitment of their people, both during and after implementation. At the same time managers often also have to ensure that business continues as usual. The second most common key reason for problems, given by over two-thirds of our organisations, was resistance to change.

Implementing strategic change is one of the most important undertakings of an organisation. Successful implementation of strategic change can reinvigorate a business, but failure can lead to catastrophic consequences, including an organisation's collapse (Hofer and Schendel 1978). Organisations and business preference often maintain the status quo, thereby ignoring the necessity to change and adapt to shifting conditions, which is yet another reason for unsustainability. For example, the 2010 Toyota product recall is an indication to the fact that the organisation failed to change internally with respect to its fast business growth, consequently affecting its current and future prospects. For example, 'Quite frankly, I fear the pace at which we have grown may have been too quick. We pursued growth over the speed at which we were able to develop our people and our organisation. I regret that this has resulted in the safety issues described in the recalls we face today, and I am deeply sorry for any accidents that Toyota drivers have experienced' (in Puzzanghera and Muskal 2010:1), said Akio Toyoda, the

President of Toyota in a statement acknowledging his company's inability to change with the pace of growth from its global expansion.

Organisational sustainability can be achieved through adapting to changes; although an organisation can only adapt through the changes when people in the organisation believe in the worthiness of the change and channel their energy in a single direction. Sustaining through people is, thus, the key organisational sustainability. We can see this in the example of AP Communications, as noted in the text box below.

Text Box 4.2: AP Communications: sustaining through people

'Business sustainability is about continuity and growth. This concept is linked to people, as it is the people that make businesses sustainable. To sustain in the long-run is to also survive by meeting the challenges of today.'
   Ms Mable Chan, Associate HR Director, AP Communications, Singapore.

Sources: Interactions with Ms Mable Chan during focus group discussion (2009) and subsequent e-mail correspondence.

Systems thinking has been defined as an approach to problem solving, by viewing 'problems' as parts of an overall system, rather than reacting to a specific part, outcome or event and potentially contributing to the further development of unintended consequences. Systems thinking is not just one thing, but rather a set of habits or practices. It is as if people of different opinions, thoughts and values are sailing a boat and discover holes in it when many of them are less bothered than the rest as the holes are not at their end of the vessel. Since their opinions are divided and priorities are different people spend their time disagreeing and opposing one another's opinion, leaving the boat to sink while they are unaware of it. Just like the people on the boat, organisations whose cultures do not promote unified thought and actions are vulnerable to sinking. Many of our organisations, nearly half, indicated the tendency of 'not being a systems thinker' or lack of systems thinking culture in the organisation as the third major reason for business unsustainability.

Forrester (in Rasmussen et al. 2007: 15) argues that risk ignorance results in an 'iceberg of risk', where the full risk exposure of the organisation is underwater and cannot be seen. A lack of executive commitment to risk management is a primary contributor to the relative immaturity of risk management in many organisations. While the involvement of senior management is arguably critical to the success of any initiative, it is absolutely essential for risk management. The reason is simple – certain aspects of risk management run counter to human nature. When an organisation attains the highest level of maturity it typically requires that dedicated resources for risk management be integrated into business processes through a formalised procedure. However, many organisations have grown an internal maze of assessments as individual responses to various risks while omitting or misaligning the strategic risk (Maziol 2009). Ignoring risks or risk ignorance is the failure of an organisation to recognise that a risk exists. Risk ignorance as a reason why businesses fail was the fourth major reason, given by just over one-third of our organisations.

Greed is an excessive desire to acquire or possess more than what one needs or deserves, especially with respect to material wealth. Freud argued that greed was natural, that man was born greedy and that tendency had to be socialised (Coutu 2003). Krugman (2002: 1) noted that the notion that 'greed is good' for society may contain a fatal flaw as: 'A system that lavishly rewards executives for success tempts those executives, who control much of the information available to outsiders, to fabricate the appearance of success. Aggressive accounting, fictitious transactions that inflates sales, whatever it takes.' Greed was the fifth major reason for problems, given by over one-quarter of our organisations.

Key measures taken

There is no escaping the harsh reality that organisations faced during the post-2008 economic crisis. Essentially, organisations had the choice to react in three different ways: offensive; defensive; do nothing. Organisations that did nothing to adapt to the changing environment and waited for the business environment to stabilise were the most vulnerable when compared with the rest. The key measures taken by organisations ranged between being defensive to offensive. In terms of our organisations, the nine measures given are listed in Table 4.4.

The top trio of measures taken by our organisations were: cost-management (nearly nine out of ten); focus on customer delight (over four-fifths); and talent management (nearly three-quarters). The next most important set of measures taken by organisations were: focus on innovation and identifying niches (well over a half); and regular communication with employees (given by just over a half). The number of organisations using other measures then fell substantially. These were: focus on learning and development and getting ready for the future (less than one-sixth); and constantly monitoring market conditions (less than one-sixth). Indeed,

| Table 4.4 | Key measures taken by organisations (n = 50) | |

Rank	Key measure	Responses (%)
1	Cost-management	86
2	Focus on customer delight	82
3	Talent management and succession planning	72
4	Focus on innovation and identifying niches	57
5	Regular communication with employees	52
6	Focus on learning and development and getting ready for future	14
7	Constantly monitoring market conditions	14
8	Efforts to keep products and services affordable	2
9	Efforts to learn from the past	2

Source: SHRI (2009)

the final two measures were given by very low numbers of organisations and concerned efforts to: keep products and services affordable (just 2 per cent); and learn from the past (just 2 per cent). We revisit some of these findings in more detail next and supplement them with further earlier research.

About nine out of ten of our organisations concentrated on cost-management through a series of procedures, reports and monitoring expenses. Efforts were made to manage investments, control variable costs and explore opportunities for savings. When asked whether cost-management was critical only during troubled times like recessions, some organisations stated that in good times competition can inflate labour costs. For example, companies in their rush to attract talent in the right place and at the right time had to increase their compensation structure so as to make it look more lucrative than their competitors rewards. Competitors then joined this 'race', in turn leading to wage cost inflation. Of course, some forward thinking strategies to retain people during recessions (see later examples), would assist in helping better control such trends and short-term behaviours (see Rowley 2010a).

The economic recession challenged organisations to maintain business operations while budgets were shrinking. Organisations were concerned that this could result in more negative customer sentiment. Many (over four-fifths) of our organisations provided additional services to delight customers and retain them. For example, some organisations maintained contacts and regularly sent appreciations of their support.

A large majority (nearly three-quarters) of our organisations identified talent management and succession planning as key measures. This is a key, integral HRM policy and practice area.

Maintaining R&D investment levels for organisations during a recession can obviously be difficult, yet it is precisely such a commitment to R&D that can be essential to an enduring competitive edge. As pointed out by the Director of Tourism for International Markets, Innovation Norway: 'It does not need to be anything big, it could be small scale. You have to challenge how things are working. But standing still is much riskier than changing' (*Travel Weekly* (UK) 2009: 1). Many of our organisations, well over a half, focused more than they did before on innovation and identifying niches.

Many (over half) of our organisations increased the frequency of communication with employees. For example, a giant food and beverage company in Singapore started organising 'chit-chat' sessions to gather feedback from employees on their work environment, policies and people matters. Similarly, a large telecom company initiated two-way conversations using social media. As the Managing Director, Marketing and Communications, Citi Global Wealth Management notes: 'In difficult times, employees may display fears about losing their jobs; be cynical or suspicious about management's motives; and demonstrate a loss of confidence in the company's overall health. As employees were critical to all communications efforts, as their conduct and confidence affected both other internal as well as external stakeholders, it was imperative that they were actively engaged' (in IPRS 2009: 1).

How organisations reacted to the post-2008 crisis in relation to employees can also be seen in an earlier research and a survey (SHRI 2008) – shown in Table 4.5. This also supports some of our research. While organisations note six measures, ranging from retrenchment to training employees for the future and looking at alternative arrangements for retaining jobs, no single measure was particularly common.

As we can see, even the top two reactions were only mentioned by about one-third of organisations – these were to retrench employees (just over one-third) and cut costs (under one-third). Nevertheless, the economic crisis lowered demand for products and services, which impacted on employment as retrenching employees became a more common measure. However, the practice of employee retrenchment is a double-edged sword.

Table 4.5   Company reactions during the post-2008 economic crisis (n = 635)

Rank	If your company's business is not doing well in times of economic downturn, what will your company do?	Responses (%)
1	Retrench employees	34
2	Cut costs	30
3	Freeze wage increases	18
4	Internally train and prepare employees for the next economic boom	14
5	Sub-contract employees to other companies	3
6	Outplace employees and help them start their own business	1

Source: Adapted from SHRI (2008)

On the one hand, it helps to ease an organisation's cost pressure; on the other hand it may badly affect the employer brand. This problematic impact was given by nearly four-fifths of organisations in other earlier research and a survey (see Table 4.6). Of course, there are other important impacts too.

In terms of other reactions by organisations in the survey (SHRI 2008), less than one-fifth mentioned freezing wages, and less than one-sixth training and preparing employees ready for the upturn. There were very few instances of the other measures. For example, very low numbers (just 3 per cent) of organisations noted sub-contracting of employees to others or outplacement and helping start their own business (just 1 per cent). Nevertheless, we can note some examples of these later measures. For example, as noted during a SHRI networking event, a Japanese MNC in the electronics manufacturing sector introduced the interesting practice of sub-contracting their employees or encouraging them to set up their own businesses related to the company's products and to be a party to the company's value chain. Another Indian IT services MNC offered employees opportunities to work with a non-profit organisation for a year while receiving half their salary. Through such practices these organisations were trying to better ensure that they were retaining their talent pool and keeping in touch with their employees, even when times were bad. These organisations believe such

Table 4.6 Effects of retrenchment on employer brand (n = 409)

Do you think retrenching employees in times of recession would affect employer brand?		
1	Yes	79%
2	No	17%
3	Not sure	4%

Source: Adapted from SHRI (2008)

activities are futuristic in nature; enabling them to portray their loyalty to employees, breeding commitment, strengthening employer brands and helping to retain their talent pool. In short, these organisations believe that one of the best ways to manage talent is to be compassionate in times of need and establish an emotional bond with employees. Importantly, such low figures (as shown above) also need to be seen in conjunction with the earlier points, such as complaints about wage cost inflation, and are a clear indication of the costs of short-term views by organisations.

The remaining measures taken by our organisations were far less common, and ranged from less than one-sixth concerned with either learning and development and getting ready for the future or monitoring markets; down to just 2 per cent making efforts to train and/or remain afloat.

Risk management strategies

Risk management is the active process of identifying, assessing, communicating and managing the risks facing an organisation to ensure that our an organisation meets its objectives. Some of the key measures that organisations started taking during the post-2008 recession also featured in their list of risk management strategies (see Table 4.7).

Cost-management (noted by over nine out of ten), talent management and succession planning (four-fifths) and focusing on innovation and operational excellence (nearly two-thirds) are by far the top three risk management strategies adopted by our organisations in order to remain sustainable. We detail further aspects of these findings next.

By cost-management organisations meant better inventory management and control, reducing wastage and producing cost-effective products and services. Cost-management as a

Table 4.7	Risk management strategies adopted by organisations (n = 50)	

Rank	Risk management strategy	Responses (%)
1	Cost-management (including producing cost-effective products/services, better inventory management and control)	92
2	Talent management and succession planning (including training locals to reduce dependency on foreign workers)	80
3	Focus on innovation and operational excellence	62
4	Exploring new market segments	40
5	Constant focus on cash flow	12
6	Reducing cost of energy and exploring alternative sources of energy	6
7	Forming strategic partnership/mergers/ acquisition	6
8	Knowledge management initiatives	2
9	Introduced business continuity plan	2

Source: SHRI (2009)

risk management strategy was by far the most commonly noted and was clearly ranked first, as most (over nine-tenths) of our organisations mentioned this.

In many parts of the world, talent management and succession planning has been one of the prominent agendas for organisations, including those operating in Asia. This area includes the idea of training locals to reduce dependency on foreign workers. We can see similar attempts in the Middle East, such as trying to make better use of graduate women (Rowley et al. 2010). Low fertility rates and an ageing population, as in many countries, prompted many organisations in Singapore to open their doors to more foreign workers, as we noted in earlier chapters. By February 2010 foreign workers comprised almost a third of Singapore's total workforce (AFP 2010). This increasing dependence on foreign workers, coupled with socio-economic changes such as an ageing workforce, led to recent changes in legislation. Singapore is taking action to slow down the hiring of foreign workers by raising the FWL. As the Finance Minister said: 'We should moderate the growth of the foreign workforce and avoid a continuous increase in its proportion of the total workforce. There are social and physical limits to how many more (foreign workers) we can absorb. But instead of imposing quotas, the government will raise the levies paid by companies for every worker they hire. This allows the foreign workforce to fluctuate across the economic cycle and enables employers who are doing well and need more foreign workers to continue to hire them rather than be constrained by fixed quotas' (AFP 2010: 1).

Such an increase in the FWL will have an immediate impact on labour-intensive industries, such as the marine sector, construction, etc, which hire large numbers of foreign workers. While industry associations are regularly in touch with the government to further discuss the challenges and seek help, many organisations, especially in the marine sector, have started training locals to reduce dependency on foreign workers, but this will take some time to work its way through. As such, this situation highlights some of the issues of allowing unrestricted migration in terms of creating 'moral hazard' and actually encouraging organisations not to invest to train and upgrade their human capital, workforce and business. Some four-fifths of our organisations gave the risk management strategy of talent management and succession planning.

Due to the small market size in Singapore, economies of scale are important for commercial viability of capital intensive businesses (MDA 2008). With limited internal consumption power and controlled markets, the local market is relatively smaller than in many neighbouring nations. In order to balance small market size and increases in productivity, many organisations focus on innovation and operational excellence. For example, Singapore Airlines is one of the companies that has been profitable every year since its inception. It achieves such a feat by improving operational excellence through some of the tactics like continuous training of its employees, consistent and continuous internal as well as external communications, and so on. The airline is also known for its innovative new approaches to customer engagement, like fax machines on board, 'book the cook' services for special meals in First and Business class, phone, fax and e-mail check-in, to list just a few (Kaufman 2010).

Various initiatives are being taken by the government to promote innovation and operational excellence among organisations. For example, SMEs in the manufacturing sector seeking to raise productivity and capability are able to benefit from the recently launched 'SME Manufacturing Excellence Programme'. This was designed and developed by the Agency for Science, Technology and Research's own Singapore Institute of Manufacturing Technology (SIMTech) to groom a pool of process improvement champions or 'TechnoVation Managers'. The programme aims to train managers in operations management innovation (OMNI). With knowledge and skills acquired from the programme, SME managers can help raise productivity and improve business and operational excellence within their companies. In addition to undergoing classroom training, trainees have the opportunity to apply the OMNI methodology to address specific operational challenges in their companies, under the mentorship of SIMTech's trainers. Companies sending their managers to the programme enjoy 70 per cent course fee funding support, plus an absentee payroll (AP) grant from the Workforce Development Agency (WDA), a statutory body under the Ministry of Manpower, Singapore. The AP grant helps companies defray the costs incurred when they send employees for training. From 2009 the AP cap for training courses under the Skills Programme for Upgrading and Resilience was revised upwards to a single rate of S$10 per hour, which translates to a maximum AP claim of about S$1,600 a month per worker (MOM 2009: 1). Over the next 2–3 years WDA and SIMTech aim to train a pool of 150 such managers to champion and lead operational improvements in their organisations (ACN 2010). Nearly two-thirds of our organisations listed the risk management strategy of focus on innovation and operational excellence.

Apart from the above trio of strategies, the fourth risk management strategy our organisations listed was: exploring new market segments and trying to reach out to newer geographical territories (by two-fifths). Beyond these four risk management strategies, the remaining five were not that commonly given by our organisations. A constant focus on cash flow was noted (by less than one-eighth), but very few of our organisations were either reducing energy costs and looking at alternative sources (only 6 per cent), or forming strategic partnerships and M&A (6 per cent), with even fewer of our organisations introducing business continuity plans (just 2 per cent) or knowledge management initiatives (2 per cent). This last strategy's very low level is very surprising given the importance of the latter area and its critical role in the development, upgrading and adding value of businesses and economies (Rowley and Poon 2010a).

Future challenges

Business sustainability seeks to create long-term shareholder value by embracing the opportunities and managing the risks that result from an organisation's TBL of economic, environmental and social responsibilities. Thus, business sustainability can be described as the application of knowledge, skills, tools and techniques to the organisation's activities, products, and services in order to accomplish an organisation's vision and mission.

Regardless of how large or how profitable they are, many organisations are inextricably linked with the societies in which they operate. This is not least because every decision they make, whether it is to close a plant, relocate operations or develop or set a price for new products, will eventually affect the surrounding community and the natural environment, for better or for worse. Furthermore, many MNCs use emerging markets as a part of their production chain, which is especially true for the Asian economies (Korhonen and Fidrmuc 2010). The global economy is driven by increasing technological scale, connections between firms and information flows (Kobrin 1997: 147–8) and is one 'with the capacity to work as a unit in real time on a planetary scale' (Castells 1996: 92).

In this increasingly wired world, organisations operating in one part of the world impact on others even though they are geographically located far away from one another, even in other continents. Thus, on one hand the business world has become 'glocalised' – having the ability to think globally and act locally, while on the other hand the number of variables affecting business sustainability has multiplied, making it more complex than ever before. ·

By and large organisations perceive the future to be uncertain. Having identified nine key challenges (see Table 4.8) that they think will affect their businesses over the next five years, organisations are looking to find suitable solutions. We detail these further next.

There are three socio-economic forces driving possible talent shortages: demographic decline in many nations; a skills gap because students and workers are not receiving the education and training needed for high-tech

Table 4.8	Greatest challenges for organisations over the next five years (n = 50)

Rank	Greatest future challenges	Responses (%)
1	Talent management	86
2	Understanding customers' expectations	72
3	Leadership development	62
4	Innovating new products and services	58
5	Financial viability	46
6	Venturing into new market	40
7	Business transformation and developing new business model	34
8	Manage and motivate employees	18
9	Energy usage and waste management	4

Source: SHRI (2009)

employment (human capital issues); and a cultural bias against undertaking the rigorous educational preparation needed for scientific or technical employment (Gordon 2009). It is no surprise that talent management tops the list of challenges that the vast majority (nine in ten) of our organisations foresee.

With globalisation and frequent inflow and outflow of consumers from one geographical location to another, the customer landscape has become more challenging for organisations and doing business. Adding to this are new social media like Facebook, Twitter etc. and forms of networking between customers. Customers keep getting connected, but often more to each other than those that they buy from (IBM 2010). This situation requires the formation of a bond between the customer and the provider. Hence, understanding customer expectations is going to be one of the critical challenges for organisations in the future. The challenge of understanding and meeting customer expectations was noted by nearly three-quarters of our organisations, the second most commonly noted issue.

The talent crisis may lead to the slower growth of an organisation due to unfilled positions, but a shortage of leaders with the right abilities can cause a firm's demise. Leadership development is also a challenge elsewhere in Asia and around the world (see Rowley and Poon 2010b). One study notes that about two-thirds of the companies surveyed said the lack of leadership talent was having a moderate to major impact on their ability to achieve business goals (Executive Development Associates 2005). Some additional consequences of such shortages include increased spending on recruitment and training and the intangible costs of poor decision-making as companies fill positions with people who are less qualified. In fact, leadership development is another significant challenge for our organisations, and indeed was the third most common, noted by nearly two-thirds.

With high customer expectations, innovating new products and services will remain a challenge for organisations. Indeed, this issue was given by well over half of our organisations, making it the fourth most common challenge.

While investing in R&D for new products and services, organisations also expect challenges to ensuring financial viability. This issue was given by under half of our organisations, the fifth most common challenge.

With highly competitive local markets and market saturation, organisations will have to look beyond local geographical borders to venture into new markets. Indeed, two-fifths of our organisations expect to face issues related to this, making it the sixth most common challenge.

These challenges include identifying and understanding new markets, assessing the feasibility of doing business there, arranging initial capital for such expansion, getting people on board with skills suited to such new markets and more. These trends will require the development of new business models. Indeed, just over one-third of our organisations noted this, making it the seventh most common challenge.

A business in transformation is complex to manage. Adapting to new business conditions requires a pool of motivated employees who will have trust in the organisation and firm belief in its direction. Yet, post-2008 downturn employees have become more sceptical about business decisions. Thus, organisations may anticipate a challenge in restoring such beliefs to surge ahead with a team of motivated employees. Less than one-fifth of our organisatons mentioned such issues, making it the eighth most common challenge.

It is often asserted that energy usage and waste management will be one of the greatest future challenges for organisations. It is interesting to note that only a very small number of our organisations (just 4 per cent) listed this issue, making it only the ninth challenge. Is this low position due to ignorance or contentment? Or could it be that organisations are yet to catch up with the 'going green' mission? Whatever the reason, it is a somewhat surprising result.

Conclusion

In this chapter we have examined organisational views and business sustainability in terms of: core values, key challenges, reasons for unsustainability, measures taken, risk management strategies, and future challenges. What we found was that business sustainability still seems to be a maze for many organisations. Irrespective of their size, the organisations covered in this book vary along the sustainability continuum, of between not being sustainability aware to mature sustainability leaders. Though many organisations are aware that adopting practices balancing the 3Ps of people, prosperity and planet dimensions will help them ensure greater business sustainability, they are often stuck in the quagmire of achieving just-in-time, visible and countable benefits and hence short-termism and its consequent behaviours and actions, which may come at a cost, not least the long-term survival of the organisation and types of HRM practices, are adopted.

Interestingly, there were many key HR issues mentioned by our organisations. These included the key challenges faced, where two of the nine were key HR-related issues – ranked third (by 62 per cent, employee engagement) and fifth (by 6 per cent, work-life balance); while two of the nine key measures taken were HR-related issues – ranked third (by 72 per cent, talent management) and fifth (by 52 per cent, employee communication). Of the nine risk management strategies, two were HR-related – ranked second (by 80 per cent, talent management) and eighth (by 2 per cent, knowledge management). Of the nine future challenges, three were HR-related – ranked first (by 86 per cent, talent management), third (by 62 per cent, leadership development) and eighth (by 18 per cent, managing and motivating employees). These findings echo earlier, similar, research (SHRI 2008) where all six reactions of organisations to economic crisis were HR-related. The critical role of HR to organisations remains unabated and even seems to be more important as a result of the impacts of the post-2008 economic crisis.

The next chapter illustrates some of the innovative, sustainability-oriented practices adopted by some organisations, including in HRM. It also provides an integrated framework and suggests a road towards a more sustainable future.

5

Towards a business sustainability future

Abstract: What will a sustainable future look like? Will it be devoid of uncertainties? Can we take informed decisions today to stabilise future uncertainties if they arise? Did organisations learn any lessons from the crises and set out a framework for business sustainability? What actions need to be taken today in order to progress towards a more sustainable future? Will ethics play any role in the sustainability of a business or will the corporate world ignore any conscience factor? This chapter elaborates further on these points and uncovers the factors responsible for future uncertainties, sustainability initiatives taken by a few organisations, and enumerates a framework for business sustainability.

Key words: uncertainty, sustainability initiatives, framework for business sustainability, talent management, innovation, risk management, Integrated Model of Business Sustainability, sustainability awareness, innovative sustainability initiative.

Introduction

As the essence of business sustainability is now clearer than before, a set of questions arises. What will a sustainable future look like? Will it be devoid of uncertainties? Can we take informed decisions today to stabilise future uncertainties if they arise? Did organisations learn any lessons from the post-2008 crises and set out a framework for business sustainability? What actions need to be taken today in order to progress towards a more sustainable future? Will ethics play any role in the sustainability of a business or will the corporate world ignore any conscience factor?

The following statement by UNESCO also raises such questions about the 'sustainability of sustainability' and indicates that businesses should to look again into the areas of ethics and morality: 'Perhaps we are beginning to move towards a new global ethic which transcends all other systems of allegiance and belief, which is rooted in a consciousness of the interrelatedness and sanctity of life. Would such a common ethic have the power to motivate us to modify our current dangerous course? There is obviously no ready answer to this question, except to say that without a moral and ethical foundation, sustainability is unlikely to become a reality', UNESCO (1997: para 116).

This chapter will elaborate further on these points. These cover: future uncertainties; sustainability initiatives; and a framework for business sustainability. Along the way we present and use another set of seven diverse case studies/ vignettes to help bring the work to life. A conclusion brings this chapter to a close.

Future uncertainties

Uncertainty is a state of having limited knowledge about present or future outcomes. It may manifest itself in varied dimensions, from affecting macro-economic stability to intra-organisational dynamisms. With dynamic business environments and multiple variables, organisations around the world encounter the challenge to recognise uncertainty and take remedial measures on time, every time. During a conversation with the British Prime Minister on how to make society more robust (that is, more tolerant of unexpected events), it was noted that that we are living in a world that is extremely different from that we inherited from the past (Taleb 2009). Now rumours are global and we are much more vulnerable to extreme deviations. It was also indicated that globalisation has made companies very efficient, yet very fragile (Taleb 2009). With the ever increasing use of IT, the speed of interactions and reactions has become remarkably fast-paced. Due to the tools we have in our hands, we can no longer make the same mistakes that we have done in the past (Taleb 2009). In other words, the frequency of uncertainties in the business environment have increased manifold with an ever increasing need to carefully look once more into the core components of business sustainability in order for an organisation to stay sustainable during the karmic phase and beyond.

Much uncertainty is not introduced by the marketplace, but is rather system induced, that is, it germinates within the organisation due to the various internal dynamics it has within its processes, policies and practices. It is then magnified by the 'bullwhip effect' (a term indicating the way the amplitude of a whip increases down its length). This concept of amplification is aptly observed in supply chains whereby unpredictable elements introduced by human behaviour in the lower part of the chain become more pronounced the higher up the chain they move (Lee et al. 1997). This effect is important because it is frequently the cause of serious inefficiencies that result from ordering too much or too little of a given product as links in the chain over-react to changes further downstream (Baugher 2010: 1).

Hence, the best way to cope with uncertainty is to work hard to reduce it (Jones and Towill 2000). Those organisations who understand the principles of uncertainty and act proactively to cope with it, often survive and sustain better than the rest. For instance, as noted by Mr Sim Kah Bin, Logistics Department, SE Net Fashion Development Pte Ltd, Singapore, some businesses fail to unlearn what they have learnt and do not know how to relearn (SHRI 2009).

A business cannot prosper over the long term without the capacity to manage risks and uncertainties. It will stumble from crisis to crisis, but it will not survive and it will fail. Risk and uncertainty have real impacts on earnings, cash flow and shareholder value. They cut across all that a business must do in order to succeed (Csiszar 2008: 3). However, though uncertainty is a phenomenon experienced by all businesses, its magnitude may vary across industries and over time.

How then can businesses reduce uncertainty and thrive over time? In times of crisis, panic sets in and more often than not businesses tend to ignore the fundamentals. There are a few elements which are fundamental and work in most situations to reduce uncertainty. First, there is the regular analysis of what is working and what is not. Second, assessing new ways to control the quality and price of products and services is needed. Third, creating a 'win-win' proposition for all stakeholders is commonplace. The success of the above elements depends in turn mostly on senior management's clarity of thought and vision, ability to take unbiased decisions in both good or difficult times and the willingness of the organisation to undergo Schumpeterian 'creative destruction' (Schumpeter 1942). The following section highlights examples of some innovative business sustainability initiatives implemented by organisations in various parts of the world.

Innovative sustainability initiative

Innovation is a change in the thought processes for doing something, or the useful application of new inventions or discoveries (Barras 1984). Innovation is at the core of business sustainability. Interestingly, the very vision of an organisation's sustainability can be a strategic trigger to innovation. Innovation may be incremental, evolving or revolutionary changes in processes, products, services or organisations with the underlying objective of staying relevant in the present and sustainable in the future.

Is innovation an indispensable platform for brand positioning? Examining the examples of Make Health Connect (MHC) Asia Group Pte Ltd, Singapore's COFFEE BEAN and Korean Air, spreading the green message project can help to shed light on the question. We detail these next in our short case studies and vignettes.

Case Study 5.1: MHC: The COFFEE BEAN Project

Established in 1996, MHC operates in the healthcare sector, offering web based information systems for historical data of health and disease patterns of an organisation's workforce. This less than 50 employee SME also offers third party administration and consultancy services related to employee health to design and customise health care plans. The healthcare sector was not hit that much by the post-2008 economic downturn, but still faced challenges due to the need to contain costs. This innovative MHC venture – The COFFEE BEAN Project – is worth mentioning as to how a simple looking effort can bring long-lasting benefits.

MHC adopted the acronym COFFEE BEAN – Comfort Our Friends, Fill Each Emptiness. Be Encouraging And Nice. The project was an effort to primarily help Singaporeans hit hard by the post-2008 economic crisis. People lost their jobs and savings and so were in dire need of help. For example, during the downturn a total of S$20,000 was contributed by MHC, together with its staff and management team, to help the needy pay part of their outpatient bills. The sum of money raised was apportioned into a thousand S$20 vouchers and distributed to the needy. MHC also donated a van for a children's home in Batam, Indonesia. All promotional materials were designed and printed in-house by MHC to ensure that every dollar went to the needy.

Representatives of MHC proudly state the philosophy behind the COFFEE BEAN project as follows: 'When boiled, an egg hardens and resists changes while a carrot softens and succumbs easily to external stress. But coffee beans emit an aroma which inspires and the caffeine acts as a stimulant which refreshes the depressed soul and the spirit' (MHC 2010: 1). The project is their effort to help the underprivileged to better fight challenges, leading to collective sustenance. Thus, 'Together, we can make a difference and that is what we believe is business sustainability!' notes a senior manager from MHC. In appreciation of this initiative, the drug company Glaxo Smith Kline donated S$10,000 to the project. MHC also received notes of appreciation from their stakeholders and the brand was boosted in the minds of many people.

Sources: Interactions with the General Manager-HR and senior management, MHC Asia Singapore during focus group discussion (2009) and subsequent e-mail correspondence, MHC (2010).

Case Study 5.2: Korean Air: spreading the green message

Korean Air was established in 1969 with a vision to be a respected leader in the world airline industry. Since its incorporation it has grown tremendously, to over 19,000 employees and business operations spread over 39 countries and 117 cities. In 2009 Korean Air celebrated its 40th anniversary. During this occasion it revealed its 'Vision 2019' and the new slogan 'Beyond 40 Years of Excellence'; a vision that the airline wishes to achieve by the time it celebrates half a century of its existence. As a part of their Vision 2019, Korean Air says it will continue its 'green' efforts to help preserve and sustain the global environment. It is bringing in a unique eco-friendly management system in its bid to cut down on the environmental impact of air travel. It aims to pursue such eco-friendly management through planting trees around the world, adding more fuel-efficient aircraft to its fleet and executing campaigns to promote protecting the environment.

In 2010 one such green campaign to raise public awareness and to educate the next generation was Korean Air's appointment of a 'teddy bear crew' – one pilot-style teddy bear dubbed Mr Greene and another flight attendant-style teddy bear called Miss Love, which were to be seen as ambassadors to spread the green message. Starting from the Hong Kong regional office of Korean Air, the teddy bear ambassadors travelled around the world, to China, Korea, the UK, Spain, France, Japan and other locations, so as to publicise the eco-friendly message among the public by sharing information about the benefits of being eco-friendly. Also, internally, Korean Air is pushing a campaign to raise awareness about environmental protection among all company employees. The 'Ecoffice' campaign includes the 'Save Paper Competition' participated in by 32 departments and 'Green Day,' the last Friday of each month when employees work on different environmental themes.

Sources: Freesun News (2009); Korean Air (2010); Aviation Record (2010); Da-ye (2010).

Sustainability of its workforce is critical to driving a high-performing organisation. High-performing businesses stay relevant at any time by being innovative and retaining stakeholders' trust. Such organisations consistently outperform their competitors, bringing in economic prosperity and market leadership. These organisations concurrently work toward business sustainability goals while aptly investing in their people. For example, Tata Group testifies to the significance of people and their management, especially talent management and succession planning, in the sustainability of an organisation. We can see this next in the case study.

Case Study 5.3:   Tata: sustaining the talent pipeline

This 140-year-old Group is one of India's biggest and most respected business organisations. The Group operates in seven core business sectors: (1) communications and IT; (2) engineering; (3) materials; (4) services; (5) energy; (6) consumer products; (7) chemicals, with total revenues of US$70.8 billion in 2008–09. The company has sustained its corporate image of being an organisation with strong values and business ethics. For example, in the 2009 Forbes survey Tata was ranked as the 11th most reputable company in the world.

Tata Administrative Service (TAS) is a unique training programme, conceived by J.R.D. Tata, the late chairman of the Group, in the 1950s to groom some of the best young Indians and develop a pool of talent. This sustainable Group HR could then be tapped by companies across the Tata organisation. Each year young postgraduates are recruited from leading Business Schools and are put through a rigorous 12 month programme. Renamed 'Group Orientation And Learning' (GOAL), this programme emphasises structured orientation through classroom inputs and field visits. It builds TAS trainees' perspectives on Tata's core business sectors, its current and future challenges and its drive to become a truly global organisation. A seven week rural assignment exposes the trainees to community work and rural India, helping instill in them a true picture of the life of ordinary Indians.

Sources: Kneale (2009); Tata (2010).

Is it too far-fetched to advise businesses and organisations to learn business sustainability lessons from nature? Perhaps not, after years of evolution nature has learned what works and what lasts. Organisations that can look beyond the stereotypes are the ones more likely to succeed. An organisation we used in our research and one of its projects is an example – Autodesk's biomimicry project, which we present next.

Case Study 5.4: Autodesk Inc: The Biomimicry Project

Established in 1982, Autodesk is an American IT MNC with 6,600 employees worldwide. It is committed to providing software that helps customers simplify sustainable design decisions in each industry they serve. Autodesk has become the exclusive founding sponsor of AskNature.org — the world's first biomimicry design portal and database, where designers and innovators can search for nature's solutions to sustainable design challenges. This is a project of the Biomimicry Institute, founded by Janin Benyus, the author of the book *Biomimicry: Innovation Inspired by Nature* (2002).

Biomimicry (from *bios*, meaning life, and *mimesis*, meaning to imitate) is a design discipline that seeks sustainable solutions by emulating nature's time-tested patterns and strategies, for example, a solar cell inspired by a leaf. The core idea is that nature, imaginative by necessity, has already solved many of the problems that humans are grappling with, such as energy, food production, climate control, non-toxic chemistry, transportation, packaging, etc. In this project, nature is viewed as '3M':

Model: Biomimicry is a new science that studies nature's models and then emulates these forms, processes, systems and strategies to solve human problems – sustainably.

Mentor: Biomimicry is a new way of viewing and valuing nature. It introduces an era based not on what we can extract from the natural world, but what we can learn from it.

Measure: Biomimicry uses an ecological standard to judge the sustainability of innovations.

Sources: interactions with Mr Douglas Kelly, Talent Acquisition Manager, Autodesk, Singapore during focus group discussion (2009) and subsequent e-mail correspondence.

Sustainability of a business or an organisation may also be described in terms of its capability to maintain its culture, values, common beliefs and objectives. Be it a small business unit, a MNC or a country for that matter, sustainability also depends on how successfully one can 'pass the baton on' from one generation to the next to remain in existence. The examples of the sustainability of cultural heritage in Bhutan, Mitsubishi's forestry sustainability initiative and sustainability initiatives at SKF Group, exemplify these stances. We detail these in the next three cases.

Case Study 5.5: Bhutan's sustainability of cultural heritage

Bhutan is a unique country whose overall development policy is interwoven with Buddhist philosophies to achieve a balance between material and spiritual aspects of life, between 'peljor gongphel' (economic development) and 'gakid' and 'deva' (happiness and peace). The Royal Kingdom has intertwined the theme of sustainability in its four pillars of development strategy: (1) sustainable and equitable economic development; (2) ecological preservation; (3) cultural preservation; (4) good governance.

The national policies of Bhutan and its commitment to sustainable development are visible in their Vision 2020 statement: 'to raise the material well-being of all citizens and meet their spiritual aspirations, without impoverishing our children and grandchildren'. For instance, public opinion on the cultural pillar shows that there is a common understanding amongst the Bhutanese people that culture is very important as it serves to identify Bhutan as a nation state. Most people in the remote districts support cultural preservation, saying that it plays a symbolic role in Bhutanese society since it enables the people to differentiate themselves as a community from the rest of the world. Culture is also seen as unifying force, a bond between people indicating that one nation with one culture leads to a harmonious society.

Local organisations are playing an active role in sustaining and strengthening their cultural dimension. For example, the School of Fine Arts is the only institute that teaches students to learn Mahayana Buddhist culture. As Bhutan is built on this cultural identity as a sovereign and independent nation, it recognises 13 kinds of arts and crafts ('zorig chosum'). These traditions had previously been inherited through families and taught only in the monastic institutions. However, the government saw a rapid decline of these arts in recent years and only a few people possess the knowledge to preserve this heritage. For example, by 1999 only a single person who could make traditional Bhutanese boots was known to exist in the country. This master then trained six students and this has now become a regular programme. Similarly, traditional drum-making skills have been restored by recapturing the skills from the few artisans remaining in Bhutan. In recent years the enrolment rate of students has increased beyond the institute's capacity. This has ensured the sustainability of Bhutan's rich cultural heritage as it is now being passed on seamlessly from one generation to the next.

Sources: RGoB (1999: 19); Rinzin (2006: 30, 32–3).

When an organisation's top management visibly cares for sustainability and takes active measures, the essence of this can percolate across the organisation. This can be seen from the following examples of Mitsubishi Corporation and SKF Group.

Case Study 5.6: Mitsubishi: A sustainability initiative

Mitsubishi Corporation is Japan's largest general trading company with over 200 bases of operations in approximately

80 countries worldwide. As an environmentally progressive company, Mitsubishi joined a programme established by Kochhi Prefecture (one of the country's 47 sub-national jurisdictions) to promote forest restoration. Accordingly, the company will take forest land in Aki City, the birthplace of Mitshubishi founder Yataro Iwasaki, into its care, as a company-owned forest. The aim of the project is to contribute to the protection of the regional environment. In addition, a 212 hectare expanse of woodland also known as 'Yataro's Forest' is being developed as a place for the environmental education of local residents and company employees, as well as conducting forest management and maintenance initiatives. This project has been named the 'Mitsubishi Corporation Thousand Year Forest' to mark the company's efforts in contributing towards environmental sustainability.

Source: MC (2009).

Case Study 5.7: SKF: Care for sustainability – an example from China

Sustainability is a hot topic in China and organisations are pondering the benefits of business sustainability initiatives. For instance, various sustainability initiatives of the SKF Group are noteworthy in this respect.

SKF, the Swedish multinational corporation, is the leading manufacturer of roller bearings. Founded in 1907, the company grew at a rapid rate to become a global company with more than 100 manufacturing sites and is represented in more than 130 countries. SKF's sustainability efforts rest on four pillars which they call 'SKF Care': (1) business care; (2) environment care; (3) employee care; (4) community care. It has various initiatives balancing these four dimensions. For example, SKF aims to reduce waste and increase recycling for both environmental and cost reasons. For instance, in 2009 it recycled 98,000 tonnes of scrap metal from various operations and was able to reduce waste sent to landfill by more than 50 per cent between 2007–09. As part of their employee care initiative, SKF takes utmost care to provide its employees with a safe working environment and was the first major bearing manufacturer to achieve the Occupational Health & Safety Advisory Services (OHSAS) 18001 group certification in 2005, covering 82 units in 24 countries. Prevention of corruption is one of the key components of business care. Various events and activities are organised on a regular basis to spread the message of sustainability in the community.

Source: SKF (2010).

The above examples help us consolidate the ideas generated thus far into a framework of business sustainability. We detail this next.

Framework of business sustainability

The post-2008 global financial crisis induced an economic downturn that hit the business environment. Companies were challenged with managing the situation as they strived to sustain business competitiveness. The global uncertainties prompted businesses to actively focus on various alternatives to sustain themselves. We saw this in the earlier chapters of our book. Thus, there was a varied response to this scenario with organisations ranging from being well prepared to being caught by surprise. Some organisations focused exclusively on cost-cutting initiatives with rampant retrenchment, whereas a few organisations like Jason, iqDynamics or Atlas Sounds and Vision Pte Ltd executed their meticulously laid out risk management plans. Drawing from such organisational experiences, an integrated framework for business sustainability is charted here, assuming the organisation is just starting its journey afresh and wishes to remain sustainable.

Broadly speaking, an individual or a group of individuals with similar mentalities and objectives come together with a vision to start an organisation. Each organisation starts functioning through people, has processes and a purpose, needs capital and delivers products/services; in other words it creates value for its stakeholders. The organisation maintains its products/services, manages the quality and risks and innovates newer products/services when needs be. Organisations then interact with the broader business ecosystem. The key factors affecting the broader business ecosystem may then be analysed by looking into the political, economic, social, technological, environmental and legal (PESTEL) aspects.

The above key factors, if well managed, will lead to business excellence. Business excellence reduces uncertainty and over a period of time will lead to business sustainability which is depicted in the following 'integrated model of business sustainability' (see Figure 5.1). Prosperity is a consequence of people and the planet being taken good care of. The framework provides a structured approach to readers to organise their thought processes and help them to look into various parameters/factors affecting business sustainability. Further details are beyond the scope of this book.

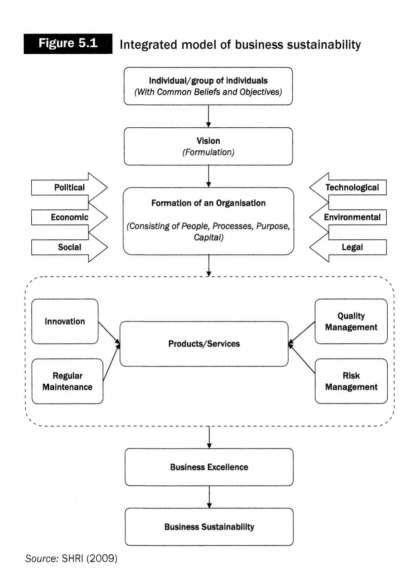

Figure 5.1 Integrated model of business sustainability

Source: SHRI (2009)

Raising awareness about sustainability

Business sustainability is a conscious decision encapsulating the '3Ps' of people, prosperity and planet. Awareness about sustainability is a basic element in the pursuit of business excellence and sustainability. Sustainability impacts work differently in various areas of an organisation. Laughlin (1991) identifies three important components within an organisation as seen in the table:

1. sub-systems

2. design archetypes

3. interpretive schemes.

Table 5.1   Laughlin's organisational elements

Components	Examples
■ Sub-systems	■ Tangible organisational elements such as buildings, people, machines, finance and behaviours
■ Design archetypes	■ Organisation structure, decision processes, communication systems
■ Interpretive schemes	■ Beliefs, values, norms, mission, purpose and meta-rules

Source: Adapted from Laughlin (1991)

Laughlin (1991) asserts that an organisation keeps functioning in a 'balanced' state of its three main organisational elements – 'subsystems', 'interpretive schemes' and 'design archetypes' – unless disturbed by external environmental turbulence, stirring its existing 'balanced' state and compelling it to adapt, reorient and/or transform itself in order to cope with the new environmental conditions. The external environmental disturbance(s) initiates a change in the organisation's 'design archetype' (the organisation structure, decision processes, communication systems), which, in turn, leads to a change in its 'interpretive schemes' (the mission/objectives, beliefs/values/norms/culture, and the organisation rules and policies) and 'sub-systems' (tangible organisational elements, like buildings, premises, machines, finances, locations) (Khan 2008).

In order to be effective, and for seamless percolation across the organisation, sustainability awareness plans must be built around each of these components. Sustainability initiatives must be tangibly visible, as in the earlier Korean Air case; they must be internalised in the organisational processes, as in the earlier Tata case and it has to be imbibed into the organisation's value system, vision and mission, as in the earlier case of Bhutan's sustainability of cultural heritage.

A targeted communications approach, that ensures that employees receive the business sustainability messages that are important to them, might be quite useful. One effective way to emphasise the relevance of sustainability to staff is to build sustainability objectives into corporate business planning and job plans. At a corporate or business level, sustainability should be outcome-focused and not solely input or process based. For instance, making sustainability part of the performance management and appraisal process can help better ensure that it is given a higher priority. It is important that employees understand what contribution they can make to the sustainability agenda. Additionally, a few organisations, like Rio Tinto (2004), now include sessions on sustainability as part of their induction programmes which are compulsory for all new employees. Awareness about sustainability can also be raised at team meetings by embedding sustainability into business planning and by encouraging staff to consider sustainability in their daily work.

Conclusion

New business infrastructure and competitive human capital within a dynamic labour market are factors that lead organisations to redefine their business strategies and enhance people management practices (Rowley and Harry 2011; Rowley and Redding 2011). Addressing these efficiently means that organisations will have to strike a balance with their limited resources and constraints as they work towards business excellence and sustainability.

Any uncertainty a business or enterprise faces will heighten the pressures for the organisation to be vigilant and creative in ensuring business viability. During such periods, productivity in general, and innovation in particular, will be the order of the day. Together with brand reputation, leaders focus on the need for creativity and reflection on the purpose, process and people of the enterprise to stay relevant and sustainable. Interestingly, The Kauffman Foundation sponsored a study that found more than half of the companies on the 2009 *Fortune* 500 list were launched during a recession or bear market (Stangler 2009). For example, it was during the Great Depression that Walt and Roy Disney founded their company Disney Brothers Cartoon Studio in 1923 (Dahl 2010).

There might be innumerable factors which will create the haze of uncertainty for businesses to thrive in the future. Assuming the future is provisional and cannot be predicted with accuracy, organisations must develop the capacity to respond to remain sustainable. Intel's Chairman warns about managerial complacency (Grove 1998), as indicated by the use of the word 'paranoid' in the title of his book. This asserts that by adopting a state of watchfulness an organisation can be in a better position to pick up on unplanned and unexpected change and sees change in the business environment as a series of 'strategic inflection points' when the fundamentals by which an organisation operates change suddenly and without warning (ibid.). Yet, how can one distinguish the signals from the noise? The book suggests engaging in continuous debate and analysis, sharing information and generating new ideas as one way (ibid.). Thus, the ability for organisations to succeed or fail lies deep within their willingness to perceive the situation and act accordingly. Let the future be a choice and not a destiny for organisations and their managers.

6

Conclusion: business sustainability is beyond just lasting

Abstract: The post-2008 global financial crisis and its commensurate impacts prompted businesses around the world to re-examine their capability to be able to better survive and endure through such economic strife and chaos. This chapter reaffirms our stance and concludes that business sustainability is actually about more than just organisations lasting a long time. Rather, it is a conscious and integrated effort balancing the social, economic and environmental factors and that business sustainability is beyond just lasting!

Key words: key measures, business strategies, future challenges.

In 2008 the world experienced one of the biggest economic crises since the Great Depression – a period now infamously known as the era of the global financial crisis. This period, tainted with financial mega-scandals, has come to symbolise the height of human greed, selfishness, corporate fragility, chaos and disrespect for public well-being. The capricious capitalism and market failure was attacked from many sides. It was during this period that the stage of this book is set. Our research explored the depths and heights of business sustainability under globalisation and attempted to capture the significant moments when the crisis rocked corporate economies and boardrooms around the world.

The research was undertaken in response to a call from various corporate communities. The focus groups, interviews and case studies generated helped gather enormous insights on the topic for present and future generations to witness and act upon in terms of reinforcing business sustainability. The research helped in reinforcing, be it in such times of distress or under normal circumstances, the choice to succeed or fail which remains with the organisation. Furthermore, since the corporate atmosphere in this globalised world is so wired and connected, the cases from Singapore can be seen as representative of the patterns of corporate practices that exist in other parts of the world, albeit while carrying an Asian flavour.

The first chapter introduced the specific aims of the book, which were to highlight the perceptions of organisations on business sustainability; the challenges, issues, risk management strategies and measures these organisations used in trying to sustain themselves. Whether organisations have the courage to lead and be unique or have a 'herd mentality' – a tendency to be influenced by peers to adopt certain behaviours, follow trends and are engulfed in institutional isomporphism – is one question. DiMaggio and Powell (1983: 149) define institutional isomorphism as: 'a constraining process that forces one unit in a population to resemble other units that face the same set of environmental conditions' that result from coercive, mimetic and normative mechanisms. Whether organisations value ethics or believe in attaining their goals by hook or by crook is another question we deal with. Chapter 1 finally sets the context of this book for its readers and notes the rationale of organising the book in the way it is.

In the second chapter the book explored what business sustainability looks like under globalisation; whether globalisation has helped induce and or increase corporate fragility. It discusses the perspective that if we agree to the fact that an organisation is a living entity, can organisations then learn lessons of longevity and leave their footprints beyond their karmic phase or mere physical existence? After dealing with that idea, we then broadly explain the factors affecting sustainability of businesses while diagrammatically listing the key components of TBLs. How organisations can assess their sustainability positions by using metrics and measurements of business sustainability is also introduced. At the end of this chapter we concluded that more often than not organisations tend to focus just on being economically prosperous, thereby having a short-term vision which ultimately leads to premature organisational mortality.

In the third chapter we developed a medley of individual cases and vignettes of organisations and included their experiences and apprehensions regarding business sustainability. The cases exhibit the varied extent to which these organisations are aware of the TBLs and their respective actions. Diverse cases of SMEs, VWOs, large local firms and MNCs operating in Singapore were provided. Organisations' responses to the concept of business sustainability were varied, ranging from strengthening their internal processes, focusing on employees and investing in product innovation, to cutting costs, closing units and reducing balance sheet losses.

The fourth chapter voiced the key challenges faced by organisations during the post-2008 financial crisis and economic recession. This was in terms of: core values which organisations adhered to try to sustain; reasons cited for unsustainability; measures taken; risk management strategies adopted and future challenges identified. As listed in the chapter's tables, the key challenges faced by organisations were how, and by how much, to cut costs and how to handle situations that occurred due to budget freezes on the client side, ensuring cash flow and matters related to employee engagement and continuity of trust between employer and employees. Interestingly, poor leadership was pointed out as the key factor responsible for corporate unsustainability. Yet cost-management and control were the primary focus of these organisations during the time of crisis. These findings raised some key, but simple, questions: When times are good does the corporate sector ignore the factors responsible for business excellence and in turn invite situations that shake up sustainability? Are the talent and leadership pipelines adequate enough to share future responsibilities? If talent management is unanimously identified as the key future challenge, what are organisations doing to try to help limit and overcome this? What we found was that business sustainability still seems to be a labyrinth for many organisations, while a distinct imbalance in the TBL factors and 'the planet dimension' is yet to get up speed.

The fifth chapter discussed the above-mentioned scenarios and illustrated innovative sustainability initiatives adopted by some of the organisations we researched. Based on the insights gathered, a framework of business sustainability was charted in an effort to guide organisations' thought processes and help them to achieve greater business sustainability. Through this chapter it was further reinstated that the ability for organisations to succeed or fail lies deep within their willingness to perceive the situation and act accordingly.

While penning these chapters we were constantly confronted with the fact that sustainability is a balancing act to be judiciously executed. The essence of sustainable development is perhaps well represented through this quote: 'The genius of sustainable development is to finesse the perceived conflict between economy and environment and between the present and future' (Board of Sustainable Development 1995: 13). In other words, it can be concluded that more often than not business sustainability is a choice that germinates in corporate boardrooms, spreads across organisations through clear vision and subsequent action and is a phenomenon that is driven by human greed, lust for power and other inter- as well as intra-organisational political plays. Therefore, sustaining a business will also mean balancing power struggles and conflicts within the organisation. Business sustainability is beyond just lasting!

In short, our research and book have uncovered and analysed a plethora of ways organisations of different sizes and sectors have tried to maintain business sustainability, and what they see as some of the future challenges to this. Interestingly, many of the challenges, measures, strategies and future challenges mentioned by our organisations had a very strong HRM aspect. These areas ranged from improved employment engagement and communication and work-life balance to better talent management and succession planning as well as leadership and leadership development. We can see these in Table 6.1.

What these results also seem to indicate is that the critical role of HR in organisations remains unabated and the management of people and people issues would seem to be becoming even more important as a result of the impacts of the post-2008 economic crisis. Indeed, some important issues, such as ethics and CSR, can be colonised by HR professionals (Rowley 2010b). Furthermore, it indicates that despite a common narrow view that HRM is less important and simply an implementer of decisions made elsewhere in the organisation, the opposite may be the case. That is, it is an opportunity for HRM to show how it adds value to the organisation and can prevent it from hitting the rocks and sinking.

Table 6.1	HRM-related key challenges, measures, risk management strategies and future challenges given by organisations

Area	Topic	Percentage	Rank (out of 9)
Key challenges	Employee engagement	62	3
	Work-life balance	6	5
Measures	Talent management	72	3
	Employee communication	52	5
Strategies	Talent management	80	2
	Knowledge management	2	8
Future challenges	Talent management	86	1
	Leadership development	62	3
	Managing and motivating	18	8

Source: SHRI (2009)

Appendix:
Singapore education and
training system at a glance

The vision for Singapore is to be 'a developed country in the first league' (MTI 2000). As a small island city-state endowed with no natural resources, Singapore has had to emphasise the human skills of its population and human capital to be economically competitive. The government has, therefore, stressed education and training to enhance the competitiveness of the country.

In 2000 Singapore's Minister of Education Teo Chee Hean expressed his aspiration to make Singapore the 'Boston of the East' (Teo 2000). The education industry already formed an integral part of Singapore's economy, contributing 3 per cent to GDP in 2000 and by September 2001 there were some 50,000 foreign students on student visas. The Economic Review Committee (ERC) 2002 identified education as one of the service industries to be developed and promoted, not only to cater to local needs but also to a large number of international students studying in Singapore.

The education system in Singapore – the genesis

After the founding of Singapore by Sir Stamford Raffles of the East India Company in 1819, a dual education system developed between English-language schools and vernacular schools that taught in the mother tongue (Chinese, Malay and Tamil).

By the 1860s it was recognised that schools required financial assistance and the colonial state abandoned its non-interventionist policy by initiating a small number of English-language primary and secondary schools and providing free Malay-language primary education. Grants-in-aid were given to non-government schools but these did not begin on a regular basis until 1920 (Gopinathan 1974). The Winstedt Committee on Industrial and Technical Education (1925) was more forward-looking and highlighted the pressing demand for English-speaking clerks of works, assistant surveyors, road overseers and marine engineers (Wong and Ee 1971). The Straits and Federated Malay States Government Medical School was established in 1905 using funds raised largely by the Chinese community in Singapore and Penang. In 1921 the school was expanded and renamed King Edward VII College of Medicine. In 1929 Raffles College was established to offer courses in the arts and sciences.

After the Second World War the colonial education policy took a dramatic turn in the wake of riots and agitation, particularly among the Chinese, for an end to colonial rule. The Ten Years Program, adopted in 1947, was based on three principles (Gwee 1969):

1. education should be aimed at fostering the capacity for self-government and the idea of civic loyalty and responsibility;

2. equal opportunity for all; and

3. free primary education in English, Chinese, Malay and Tamil.

In 1948, several businesspeople recommended that a proper polytechnic should be set up to train technicians and craftsmen. The Report of the Committee on a Polytechnic Institute for Singapore (1953) recommended the establishment of a polytechnic on four grounds (Tan 1994):

- the obvious lack of technical expertise,
- the breakdown of the traditional apprenticeship system,
- the return of many European engineers to their countries after the war, and
- the difficulty in recruiting technicians from the region because immigration laws restricted entry to highly paid foreign workers.

The Singapore Polytechnic was established the following year (1954). On attaining government, the People's Action Party (PAP) based its education policy on the All-Party Committee's Report of 1956. This power struggle within the PAP between the Chinese-educated leftists and the English-educated moderates led to an acrimonious split in 1961. In addition, Malay was declared a national language in preparation for the merger with Malaya in 1963. Because of irreconcilable differences Singapore left the federation of Malaysia in 1965.

With the consolidation of power within the PAP, the English-educated professionals continued the colonial emphasis on English-language schools for another reason: to prepare Singapore for the needs of an industrial society.

In 1962 the Singapore division of the University of Malaya became the University of Singapore. Full government recognition of the degrees conferred by Nanyang University came in 1968. In the same year, the degree courses at Singapore Polytechnic were transferred to the University of Singapore, leaving the polytechnic to concentrate on diploma courses and, from 1969, certificate-level courses. Meanwhile, the Ngee Ann Kongsi (a foundation involved in educational, cultural and welfare activities in Singapore) established Ngee Ann College in 1963.

In 1979 a Council for Professional and Technical Education under the chairmanship of the Minister for Trade and Industry recommended a substantial increase in tertiary education (diploma and degree levels) to produce sufficient trained manpower for the Second Industrial Revolution. In 1980, following Sir Frederick Dainton's Report on University Education in Singapore (1979), the government merged Nanyang University and the University of Singapore to form a single, and stronger, National University of Singapore (NUS) at Kent Ridge.

In his review on Higher Education in Singapore (1989), Sir Dainton argued that, with rapid economic growth and growing demand for graduate manpower, Singapore should build two strong comprehensive universities. Consequently, Nanyang Technological Institute (NTI, established in 1981) was renamed Nanyang Technological University (NTU) in 1991. The National Institute of Education was also established as part of NTU. In 2000 the government set up a third university, the Singapore Management University (SMU), offering courses in management. Presently, the government is looking into setting up a fourth university in Singapore.

It is interesting to note that in Singapore about 65 per cent of the education establishments commenced operations in 1990. Foreign-owned organisations represented 5.9 per cent of the education sector, with an employment share of 3.5 per cent. Some of the more well-known foreign-owned education organisations in Singapore include the British Council English Language Teaching Centre (UK), University of Chicago Graduate School of Business (US) and INSEAD (France).

Singapore education system – policies and practices

The structure of the education system in Singapore is diagrammatically shown in Exhibit A.1 below. The education at all levels (primary, secondary and tertiary) is flexible and broad-based to ensure all-round or holistic development of the learners.

The Ministry of Education's 1997 mission statement, 'Thinking Schools, Learning Nation' (TSLN), has directed the transformation in the education system in recent years. Since 2003, the Ministry has focused on nurturing a spirit of innovation and enterprise (I&E). In 2004, Prime Minister Lee Hsien Loong called on the teachers to 'teach less, so that our students could learn more', which forms the basis for the TSLN. The Ministry of Education (MOE) also introduced an instructional approach, Strategies for Active and Independent Learning (SAIL) to enhance teaching and learning in schools. The SAIL approach aims to engage students in active and reflective learning, and to nurture independent learning habits (MOE 2001).

Singapore's local tertiary education institutions are unable to meet existing demand, resulting in a considerable need for international education. There are two types of

Exhibit A.1 Structure of the education system in Singapore

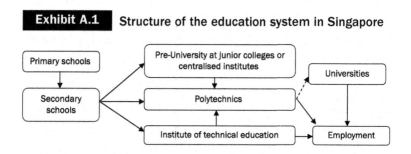

transnational education in Singapore: 'external' distance education programmes and foreign university branch campuses. External programmes are offered in Singapore by a local institution in conjunction with a foreign awarding university, and since the mid-1990s the government has encouraged a select group of elite foreign universities to offer programmes and establish centres.

Singapore has attracted 10 world-class universities, including INSEAD, Massachusetts Institute of Technology (MIT), Stanford University, Chicago Graduate School of Business, and Technische Universiteit Eindhoven.

The education market is segmented, with demand perceived to come from both consumers (students) and corporations (Singapore is a major base for the regional headquarters of multinational corporations). Singapore's education industry has progressed from supplying basic academic education to catering to varied needs ranging from personal enrichment, skills building, and professional training.

The government's annual recurrent spending on foreign students between 2005 and 2008 was estimated at about $154 million in the three publicly-funded universities and about $69 million in the five polytechnics. From 2008, fees for foreign students have been raised from 1.1 to 1.5 times local fees. This provides about one-fifth and one-tenth of the total annual recurrent grants disbursed by MOE to the universities and polytechnics respectively, and is based on the proportion of foreign students in the total student population. The funds go towards operating expenses, including staffing, equipment and other operating expenditures. In return for the subsidies they receive, foreign students are bound by the MOE's tuition grant obligation, where they have to work at Singapore-based companies for three years after graduation. Those who do not wish to meet this obligation can pay full fees with no public subsidy (MOE 2008).

Singapore Education is a multi-government agency initiative launched by the government in 2003 to establish and promote Singapore as a premier education hub and to help international students make an informed decision on studying in Singapore. This initiative is led by the Singapore Economic Development Board (EDB) and supported by the Singapore Tourism Board (STB), Standards, Productivity and Innovation Board, Singapore (SPRING), International Enterprise Singapore (IE) (all under the Ministry of Trade and Industry – MTI) and the MOE. The key roles of each agency are:

- **Singapore Tourism Board – Education Services Division**

  To promote and market Singapore education overseas

- **Singapore Economic Development Board**

  To attract internationally renowned educational institutions to set up campuses

- **International Enterprise Singapore**

  To aid quality schools to develop their businesses and set up campuses overseas

- **Standards, Productivity and Innovation Board, Singapore**

  To administer quality accreditation for private educational organisations

- **Ministry of Education**

  To oversee the public school system in Singapore.

The MTI is the most important formal institutional mechanism for governance, with the MOE and the Ministry of Manpower (MOM) following its lead, although in an integrated fashion.

Continuing education and training (CET)

As the Singapore government propounds, education will not just be about pre-work education, but also in-employment, post-work education and continuing education and training (CET) for workers at all levels, and these will become a key focus of national efforts to safeguard the employability of workers. The government has also liberalised the law to promote international cooperation in education and lifelong learning.

The government made further headway in its drive to foster a vibrant intellectual climate when Universitas 21 Global – a consortium of 21 well-known universities and Thomson Learning – established its global headquarters in Singapore in 2001. Not only is the online university the first of its kind in Asia, it adds another dimension to Singapore's global schoolhouse vision – e-learning (Yeo 2003).

Quality assurance

Singapore has an Education Excellence Framework, designed in 2004 to protect learner interests and to build high-quality education providers and which is aimed primarily at private education organisations (PEOs). The framework focuses on three key components: academic excellence, organisational excellence, and excellence in student protection and welfare practices.

The MTI has established an Education Services Accreditation Council to accredit institutions for their capabilities to deliver quality programmes. The second component of the framework focuses on enhancing the organisational excellence of the PEOs by encouraging them to upgrade through the SQC (Singapore Quality Class) for PEOs Scheme, which provides a benchmark for PEOs in business and management excellence. The third component focuses on PEOs adopting good practices in student protection and welfare through the CaseTrust for Education scheme, which includes the Student Protection Scheme.

CaseTrust is a collaborative accreditation scheme between the Consumer Association of Singapore (CASE), the Building & Construction Authority (BCA), the Economic Development Board (EDB), National Association of Travel Agents of Singapore (NATAS), Singapore Retailers Association (SRA), SPRING Singapore, Singapore Tourism Board (STB) and the Infocomm Development Authority of Singapore (IDA), supported by the MOM, for the accreditation of employment agencies and private education organisations, respectively.

Conclusion

The education system in Singapore revolves around the premise that every learner has unique aptitudes and interests and a flexible approach allows a learner to develop the potential to the fullest. In 2000 the Compulsory Education Act codified compulsory education for children of primary school age, and made it a criminal offence for parents to fail to enrol their children in school and ensure their regular attendance. Exemptions are allowed for home schooling or full-time religious institutions, but parents must apply for exemption from the MOE and meet a minimum benchmark. Special needs children are automatically exempted from compulsory education (QCDA 2008).

As can be noted from the above, Singapore has several competitive advantages that could allow it to position itself as an education hub, including its strategic geographic location, reputation for educational excellence, its vibrant business hub, and a safe and cosmopolitan environment. Singapore's education system has been described as 'world-leading' and in 2010 was among those picked out for commendation by the British education minister Michael Gove (Baker 2010).

Adapted from:

Mukherjee Saha, J. and Ang, D. (2008) 'Challenges and opportunities in the in-employment education market', Ch. 9 in Christopher Findlay and William Tierney (eds), *The Globalisation of Education: the Next Wave*, World Scientific, USA.

References

ACN Newswire (2010) 'A*STAR's SIMTech and Singapore WDA launch SME Manufacturing Excellence (S.M.E) programme', *ACN Newswire, Singapore*, 3 August 2010 viewed on 16 August 2010 <*http://www.prwire.com.au/pr/19368/a-star-s-simtech-and-singapore-wda-launch-sme-manufacturing-excellence-s-m-e-programme*>.

AFP (2010) 'Singapore to slow down hiring of foreign workers', *AFP* 22 February 2010, viewed 14 April 2010 <*http://www.google.com/hostednews/afp/article/ALeqM5gYxV7YxABU5-hIOSQLo63NKE1NYA*>.

Amin, A. and Thrift, N. (1996) (eds) *Globalisation, Institutions and Regional Development in Europe*, Oxford: OUP.

APEC (2010) 'APEC and SME POLICY: Suggestions for an action agenda', viewed 12 June 2010 <*http://www.apec.org.au/docs/iss1.htm*>.

Arizona State University (ASU) (n.d), 'School of Life Sciences (SOLS) Sustainability', viewed January 2010 <*http://sols.asu.edu/sustainability/index.php*>.

Asia Polyurethane (APU) Manufacturing Pte Ltd. (2009) *Company Profile*, Asia Polyurethane Manufacturing Pte Ltd., viewed 10 May 2009 <*http://www.apu.com.sg/profile.htm*>.

Association of Small & Medium Enterprises (ASME) (2009) *Singapore Prestige Brand Award (SPBA)*, viewed 12 May 2009 <*http://www.spba.com.sg*>.

Autodesk Inc. (2009) *Annual Report Fiscal Year 2009: Notice of Annual Meeting and Proxy statement*, Autodesk, USA.

Aviation Record (2010) *Korean Air launches sustainability initiative*, viewed 16 July 2010 *<http://webcache. googleusercontent.com/search?q=cache:f_ iUQ8J6uZAJ:www.aviationrecord.com/Cargo/tabid/68/ articleType/ArticleView/articleId/2715/Korean-Air-launches-sustainability-initiative.aspx+%22Korean+air+launches+sustainability+initiative%22&cd=1&hl=en&ct= clnk&gl=au&source=www.google.com.au>*.

Baker, M. (2010) 'Schools in a Curriculum Vacuum', *BBC News*, 18 June 2010, viewed 1 March 2011 *<http://www. bbc.co.uk/news/10355207>*.

Barney, J.B. (1991) 'Firm Resources and Sustained Competitive Advantage', *Journal of Management*, 17(1), 99–120.

Barras, R. (1984) 'Towards a Theory of Innovation in Services', *Research Policy*, 15, 161–73.

Baugher, D. (2010) *Example of the Bullwhip Effect*, eHow.com, viewed 12 October 2010 *<http://www .ehow.com/about_6367519_example-bullwhip-effect .html>*.

BBC Business News (2011) 'Singapore Economy Sees Record Expansion in 2010', 3 January 2011.

Bent, F. (2006) 'Five Misunderstandings About Case Study Research', *Qualitative Inquiry*, 12(2), April 2006.

Benyus, J. (2002) *Biomimicry: Innovation Inspired by Nature*, Perennial, USA.

Bhagwad Gita, The (n.d.) Chapter 2, Verse 22, *The Eternal Reality of the Soul's Immortality*, Bhagavad-Gita Trust, viewed 9 March 2010 *<http://www.bhagavad-gita.org/ Gita/verse-02-22.html>*.

Bhagwad Gita, The (n.d.) Chapter 2, Verse 23, *The Eternal Reality of the Soul's Immortality*, Bhagavad-Gita Trust viewed 9 March 2010 <*http://www.bhagavad-gita.org/ Gita/verse-02-23.html*>.

Biaye, M. (2010) 'Global Trends in Population Change', *LEAD International Session 2010: Population, Climate Change and Development, Port Elizabeth, South Africa, 31 October to 6 November 2010*, United National Population Fund (UNFPA), viewed 4 January 2011 <*http://southafrica2010.lead.org/wp-content/uploads/ presentation-lead_mady_biaye.pdf*>.

Board of Sustainable Development (1995) *Science for a Sustainability Transition*, 15 June 1995, National Research Council, Washington, DC.

Boston Consultancy Group (BCG) & World Federation of Personnel Management Associations (WFPMA) (2008) *Creating people advantage – How to address HR challenges worldwide through 2015*, BCG-WFPMA, USA.

Breitbart (2009) 'Over 20,000 Firms in Japan Aged 100 or Older: survey+', Breitbart, 12 August 2009, viewed 9 March 2010 <*http://www.breitbart.com/article.php?id= D9A1DDVG0&show_article=1*>.

Brundtland, G.H. (1987) *Report of the World Commission on Environment and Development: Our Common Future*, A/42/427, Oxford: OUP, viewed 16 April 2008 <*http:// worldinbalance.net/pdf/1987-brundtland.pdf*>.

Burgess, J. (2000) 'Globalisation, Non-Standard Employment and Australian Trade Unions' in C. Rowley and J. Benson (eds.) *Globalisation and Labour in the Asia Pacific Region*, London: Frank Cass, pp. 93–113.

Castells, M. (1996) 'The New Economy: Informationalism, Globalization, Networking', *The Rise of the Network Society*, Cambridge, MA: Blackwell Publishers, p. 92.

Centre For Seniors (2009) *Re-employment: Equipping and Developing Yourself (READY) TM*, Centre For Seniors, viewed 12 May 2009 <*http://www.centreforseniors.org.sg/Ready%20Promo%20Flyer%20-%206Feb09.pdf*>.

CIA (2010) *The World Factbook*, <*https://www.cia.gov/library/publications/the-world-factbook/geos/uk.html*>.

CIPD (2005) *Reorganisation will fail unless employers interact with staff to communicate the change*, viewed 10 December 2010 <*http://www.cipd.co.uk/pressoffice/_articles/07032005095612.htm?IsSrchRes=1*>.

Coutu, D. (2003) 'I was greedy, too', *Harvard Business Review*, February 2003, viewed September 2009 <*http://hbr.org/2003/02/i-was-greedy-too/ar/1*>.

Csiszar, E. (2008) 'Managing Risk and Uncertainty', *Business & Economic Review*, 55(1), 3–7.

Dahl, D. (2010) 'Top Companies Started During a Recession', *Americal Online (AOL)*, 5 October, viewed 18 November 2010 <*http://smallbusiness.aol.com/2010/05/10/top-companies-started-during-a-recession/*>.

Datamonitor (2009) *Singapore: Country Analysis Report – In-depth PESTLE Insights*, New York: Datamonitor.

Da-ye, K. (2010) 'Korean Air Fights to Reduce Carbon Footprint', *Korea Times News*, 29 September, viewed 4 October 2010 <*http://www.koreatimes.co.kr/www/news/special/2010/10/242_73718.html*>.

de Geus, A. (2002) *A Living Company*, Boston, MA: Harvard Business School Press.

de Rooij, E. (1996) *A Brief Desk Research Study into the Average Life Expectancy of Companies in a Number of Countries*, Amsterdam: Stratix Consulting Group.

Dent, C.M. (2003) 'Transnational Capital, the State and Foreign Economic Policy: Singapore, South Korea and Taiwan', *Review of International Political Economy*, 10(2), 255.

Department for Business, Innovation and Skills (BIS) (2010) 'Differences between the SME and Large Company

Schemes', viewed 12 June 2010 <*http://www.bis.gov.uk/ policies/innovation/business-support/rd-tax-credits/sme-large-company-schemes*>.

Department of Statistics, Singapore (2011) *Statistics-Economic Indicators*, Government of Singapore, viewed 18 February 2011 <*http://www.singstat.gov.sg/stats/ charts/econ.html#econC*>.

Devall, B. (2001) 'The Unsustainability of Sustainability', Culture change <*http://culturechange.org/issue19/ unsustainability.htm*>.

DiMaggio, P.L. and Powell, W.W. (1983) 'The Iron Cage Revisited: Institutional Isomorphism and Collective Rationality in Organizational Fields', *American Sociological Review*, 48(2), 147–60.

Donker, H., Poff, D. and Zahir, S. (2008) 'Corporate Values, Codes of Ethics, and Firm Performance: A Look at the Canadian Context', *Journal of Business Ethics*, Oct 2008, 82(3), 527–37.

Eaton, J.P. and Haas, C.A. (1995) *Titanic: Triumph and Tragedy*, 2nd edn, New York: W. W. Norton.

Economic Strategies Committee (ESC) Singapore (2010) *Attracting and rooting MNCs, Asian Enterprises and Global Mid-sized Companies*.

Elkington, J. (1998) *Cannibals with Forks: the Triple Bottom Line of 21st Century Business*, USA: New Society Publishers.

EnterpriseOne (2009) 'Foreign Worker Levy (FWL)', viewed 12 April 2009 <*http://www.business.gov.sg/EN/Business Topic/Hiringn/Training/EmployersResponsibilities/ TaxesLeviesNContributions/hiring_tlc_fwl.htm*>.

European Commission (2010) 'Small and Medium-sized Enterprises (SMEs)', viewed 12 June 2010 <*http:// epp.eurostat.ec.europa.eu/portal/page/portal/european_ business/special_topics/small_medium_sized_enterprises_ SMEs*>.

Executive Development Associates (EDA) (2005) *The Leadership Benchstrength Challenge: Building Integrated Talent Management Systems.*

Feng, F., Sun, Q. and Tong, W. H. S. (2004) 'Do Government-linked Companies Underperform?', *Journal of Banking & Finance*, 28(10), 2461.

Forbes (2009) 'GE Emerges World's Largest Company', *The Financial Express*, 9 April, viewed 22 December 2009 *<http://www.financialexpress.com/news/ge-emerges-worlds-largest-company-forbes/445093>*.

Freesun News (2009) *Korean Air Celebrates 40th Anniversary: 'Beyond 40 Years of Excellence'*, viewed 24 May 2010 *<http://www.freesun.be/news/index.php/korean-air-celebrates-40th-anniversary-beyond-40-years-of-excellence>*.

GE (n.d) 'Thomas Edison & GE', viewed 22 December 2009 *<http://www.ge.com/company/history/edison.html>*.

Gopinathan, S. (1974) *Towards a National System of Education in Singapore 1945–1973*, Singapore: OUP.

Gordon, E. (2009) 'The Global Talent Crisis', *Futurist*, September, pp. 35–6.

Gov Monitor (2010) 'Singapore GDP Contracts By 6.8% In The Fourth Quarter', Gov Monitor, viewed 12 November 2010 *<http://www.thegovmonitor.com/world_news/asia/singapore-gdp-contracts-by-6-8-in-the-fourth-quarter-20156.html>*.

Greiner, L.E. (1972) 'Evolution and Revolution as Organizations Grow', *Harvard Business Review*, August 1972.

Grove, A. (1998) *Only the Paranoid Survive*, illustrated, USA: Profile.

Guardian, The (2004) 'Singapore Told to Feel Free', *The Guardian*, 13 August 2004, viewed 12 November 2010 *<http://www.guardian.co.uk/world/2004/aug/13/1>*.

Gwee, Y. H. (1969), 'Education and the multi-racial society' in J.B. Ooi and H.D. Chiang (eds), *Modern Singapore*, Singapore: University of Singapore Press, pp. 208–15.

Hadiz, V. (2000) 'Globalisation, Labour and the State', in C. Rowley and J. Benson (eds), *Globalisation and Labour in the Asia Pacific Region*, London: Frank Cass, pp. 239–59.

Harcourt, T. (2000) 'Last Line of Resistance or a Golden Opportunity: Australian Trade Union Responses to Globalisation', in C. Rowley and J. Benson (eds), *Globalisation and Labour in the Asia Pacific Region*, London: Frank Cass, pp. 74–92.

Hewitt Associates (2004) 'Business Basics: People & Performance', *Hewitt Quarterly Asia Pacific*, Vol. 3.

Hirsch, S. (1967) *Location of Industry and International Competiveness*, Oxford: Clarendon Press.

Hofer, C.W. and Schendel, D. (1978) *Strategy Formulation: Analytical Concepts*, St. Paul: West.

IBM (2010) *Inheriting a Complex World: Future Leaders Envision Sharing the Planet*, IBM Global Business Services Executive Report, IBM, viewed 28 October 2010 *<ftp:// public.dhe.ibm.com/common/ssi/ecm/en/gbe03350usen/ GBE03350USEN.PDF>*.

ILO (n.d.) *Codes of Conduct for Multinationals*, viewed June 2009, *<http://actrav.itcilo.org/actrav-english/telearn/ global/ilo/guide/main.htm#Summ>*.

Institute of Public Relations of Singapore (IPRS) (2009) *Communications in the Current Financial Crisis*, viewed 20 September. *http://www.stratagemconsultants.com*.

IUCN (1994) *Guidelines for Protected Area Management Categories*, Gland and Cambridge: IUCN.

Jason Marine Group Limited (2009) *Business Excellence*, viewed 12 May 2009 *<http://www.jason.com.sg/abt_ excellence.html>*.

Jones, R. and Towill, D. (2000) 'Coping with Uncertainty: Reducing "Bullwhip" Behavior in Global Supply Chains', *Supply Chain Forum*, 1, 40–5.

Kaufman, R. (2010) 'How Does Singapore Airlines Fly So High?', viewed November 2010 <*http://www .customerservicemanager.com/how-does-singapore-airlines-fly-so-high.htm*>.

Khan, A. A. (2008) 'Paradigm Shift in the Microfinance Sector and its Implications for Theory Development: Empirical Evidence from Pakistan', *Australasian Accounting Business and Finance Journal*, 2(4), 2008, 6–30, viewed 2 February 2011 <*http://ro.uow.edu.au/ aabfj/vol2/iss4/2*>.

Kim, Jae-kyoung (2008) 'Centennial Firms Dry up in Korea', *Korea Times*, 14 May.

Kneale, K. (2009) *World's Most Reputable Companies: The Rankings*, Forbes, viewed 12 May 2010 <*http://www. forbes.com/2009/05/06/world-reputable-companies-leadership-reputation-table.html*>.

Kobrin, S.J. (1997) 'The Architecture of Globalization: State Sovereignty in a Networked Global Economy' in John H. Dunning (ed), *Governments, Globalization and International Business*, Oxford: OUP, pp. 146–7.

Korean Air (2010), 'Sustainability Management/Greetings from CEO', viewed 1 August 2010 <*http://www.koreanair.com/*>.

Korhonen, L. and Fidrmuc, J. (2010) 'The impact of the global financial crisis on business cycles in Asian emerging economies', *12th EABCN workshop on International Business Cycle – Linkages, differences and implications, Euro Area Business Cycle Network*, Budapest, 28–29 June, p. 21.

Kozul-Wright, R. (1995) 'Transnational Corporations and the Nation State', in J. Mitchie and J. Grieve-Smith (eds), *Managing the Global Economy*, Oxford: OUP, pp. 135–71.

Krugman, P. (2002),'Greed is Bad', *The New York Times*, 4 June 2002, viewed September 2009 <*http://www.nytimes .com/2002/06/04/opinion/greed-is-bad.html*>.

Laughlin, R.C. (1991), 'Environmental Disturbances and Organizational Transitions and Transformations: Some Alternative Models', *Organizational Studies*, 12(2): 209–32.

Lee, H., Padmanabhan, V. and Whang, S. (1997) 'The Bullwhip Effect In Supply Chains', *Sloan Management Review*, 38(3), 93–102.

Lee, K.Y. (2000) *From Third World to First: the Singapore Story, 1965–2000*, New York: Harper Collins Publishers.

Lepoer, L.B. (1989) (ed), *Singapore: A Country Study*, Washington, DC: GPO for the Library of Congress.

Li, X. and Rowley, C. (2005) 'Chinese SMEs', in E. Mrudla and P. Raju (eds), *China: Trading Empire of the New Century*, Hyderabad: ICFAI University Press, pp. 109–19.

Lim, H. (2009) 'Singapore's Regional Integration and Globalization Initiatives', *APEC Study Centers Consortium Conference*, 8 to 9 July 2010, Tokyo, Japan, viewed 8 May 2010 <*http://www.iseas.edu.sg/apec/ D2S10S1_Paper_Lim.pdf*>.

Lynch, P. and Rothchild, J. (2000) *One Up on Wall Street*, USA: Simon & Schuster.

Lytle, T. (2009) 'A Crisis Doesn't Always Bring Out the Best', *U.S. News & World Report*, 00415537, November 2009, Vol. 146, Issue 10.

Make Health Connect (MHC) 2010, *Coffeebeans project-A gift for the needy during the recession*, viewed June 2010 <*http://www.mhcasia.com/http:/www.mhcasia.com/mhc-news-press-release/coffeebeans-project-a-gift-for-the-needy-during-the-recession*>.

Maziol, S. (2009) *Risk Management: Protect and Maximize Stakeholder Value*, February 2009, Oracle Corporation,

USA, viewed January 2010 <*http://www.oracle.com/us/ solutions/corporate-governance/032434.pdf*>.

McNamara, C. (1999) *General Guidelines for Conducting Interviews*, Minnesota: Authenticity Consulting.

Media Development Authority (MDA) (2008) '*M1's Response to MDA's Consultation Paper on the Policy and Regulatory Framework for Mobile Broadcasting Services in Singapore*', *18 January 2008*, MDA, Singapore, viewed 28 September 2009 <*http://www.mda.gov.sg/Documents/ PDF/Reports/mobj.1183.M1.pdf*>.

Ministry of Education (MOE) Singapore (2001) *Private Schools in Singapore*, Singapore: Ministry of Education.

Ministry of Education (MOE) Singapore (2008) 'Parliamentary Replies', 21 January, viewed 14 May <*http://www.moe.gov.sg/media/parliamentary-replies/2008/01/foreign-students.php*>.

Ministry of Education (MOE) Singapore (2010) *Education Statistics Digest 2010*, Planning Division, MOE, Singapore, viewed 20 January 2011 <*www.moe .gov.sg/education/education-statistics-digest/files/esd-2010.pdf*>.

Ministry of Manpower (MOM) Singapore (2009) *Report on Labour Force in Singapore*, MOM Singapore, viewed January 2010 <*http://www.mom.gov.sg/Documents/ statistics-publications/manpower-supply/report-labour-2009/2009LabourForce_survey_findings.pdf*>.

Ministry of Trade and Industry (MTI) (2000) *The Strategic Economic Plan: Towards a Developed Nation*, Ministry of Trade and Industry (MTI), Singapore, viewed 15 February 2011 <*http://app.mti.gov.sg/data/pages/885/ doc/NWS_plan.pdf*>.

Ministry of Trade and Industry Singapore (MTIS) (n.d.) *Executive Summary – Developing Singapore's Education*

Industry, viewed 15 June 2009 <*http://app.mti.gov.sg/data/pages/507/doc/DSE_Executive%20Summary.pdf*>.

Mitshubishi Corporation (MC) (2009) *Mitshubishi Corporation (MC) Sustainability Report*, Japan.

Mukherjee Saha, J. (2009) 'The Rights' Rights and the Wrongs' Might', *Headhunt-Singapore*, 15 January, p. 8.

National Trade Union Congress (NTUC) (2010) *May Day Awards 2010*, viewed October 2010.

Practising Management Consultant Certification Board (PMCCB) (2010) *PMC NEWS – SEPTEMBER 2010*, viewed October 2010 <*http://www.pmccertboard.org.sg/newsletter/newsletter01.html*>.

Puzzanghera, J. and Muskal, M. (2010) 'Toyota President Apologizes at House Hearing', 25 February 2010, viewed 18 May <*http://articles.latimes.com/2010/feb/25/business/la-fi-toyota-hearing25-2010feb25*>.

Qualifications and Curriculum Development Agency (QCDA) (2008) 'Compulsory education, QCDA', viewed 28 November <*http://www.inca.org.uk/1018.html*>.

Ramesh, S. (2010) 'Govt's Goal is to Ensure All S'poreans Enjoy Fruits of Growth: PM Lee', 8 August, viewed 12 November <*http://www.channelnewsasia.com/stories/singaporelocalnews/view/1074117/1/.html*>.

Ramirez, C.D. and Tan, L.H. (2003) 'Singapore Inc. Versus the Private Sector: Are Government-Linked companies different?', *IMF Working Paper*, 13(156), 1–21.

Rasmussen, M., McClean, C., Penn, J. and Herald, A. (2007) *Demystifying Enterprise Risk Management – Navigating the iceberg of risk*, USA: Forrester Research Inc.

Reserve Bank of India (RBI) (2010), 'Debt Restructuring Mechanism for SMEs', viewed 12 June 2010 <*http://www.rbi.org.in/scripts/NotificationUser.aspx?Id=2502&Mode=0*>.

Rinzin, C. (2006) *On the Middle Path – The Social Basis for Sustainable Development in Bhutan*, Netherlands: Copernicus Institute for Sustainable Development and Innovation, p. 30.

Rio Tinto (2004) *Social, Safety and Environment Report 2004*, viewed 18 November 2010 <*http://www.riotinto.com/documents/ReportsPublications/02_sustainability__economic.pdf*>.

RMIT (2009) *Global Sustainability Continuum*, Melbourne: RMIT University.

RNBS (2008) *Valuing Business Sustainability: A Systematic Review*, Canada: Research Network for Business Sustainability.

Rodan, G. (1989) '*The Political Economy of Singapore's Industralization: Nation State and International Capital*', Kuala Lumpur: Forum.

Rowley, C. (2010) 'Maximizing Women's Participation in the GCC Workforce', <*http://www.cassknowledge.com/article.php?id=408&title—aximizing+women%E2%80%99s+participation+in+the+GCC+workforce*>.

Rowley, C. (1994) 'Illusion of Flexible Specialisation: The Domesticware Sector of the Ceramics Industry', *New Technology Work & Employment*, 9(2), 127–39.

Rowley, C. (1996) 'Flexible Specialisation: Comparative Dimensions & Evidence from the Tile Industry', *New Technology Work & Employment*, 11(2), 125–36.

Rowley, C. (1998) 'Manufacturing Mobility? Internationalisation, Change & Continuity', *Journal of General Management*, 23(3), 21–34.

Rowley, C. (2000) 'The Internationalization of Manufacturing: Change or Continuity?', *Global Focus: International Journal of Business, Economics & Social Policy*, 12(3), 31–40.

Rowley, C. (2003) *The Management of People: HRM in Context*, Oxford: Chandos/Spiro.

Rowley, C. (2010a) 'Employment Practices in the Recession', *Cass Knowledge*, <*http://www.cassknowledge.com/article.php?id=395&title=Employment+practices+in+the+recession*>.

Rowley, C. (2010b) 'Human Resource Management and Organisational Commitment to Corporate Social Responsibility: Examples and the Need for Context', *Cass Knowledge*, <*http://www.cassknowledge.com/article.php?id=452&title=Human+resource+management+and+organisational+commitment+to+corporate+social+responsibility%3A+examples+and+the+need+for+context+*>.

Rowley, C. and Benson, J. (2000) (eds) *Globalisation and Labour in the Asia Pacific Region*, London: Frank Cass.

Rowley, C. and Harry, W. (2011) *Managing People Globally: An Asia Perspective*, Oxford: Chandos.

Rowley, C. and Poon, I. (2010a) 'Knowledge Management', in C. Rowley and K. Jackson (eds) (2011) *HRM: The Key Concepts*, London: Routledge, pp. 142–6.

Rowley, C. and Poon, I. (2010b) 'Leadership Development', in C. Rowley and K. Jackson (eds) (2011) *HRM: The Key Concepts*, London: Routledge, pp. 151–5.

Rowley, C. and Redding, G. (2011) 'Building Human and Social Capital in Asia', *Asia Pacific Business Review*, 17, 2.

Roy, A. (2008) 'Cambridge Pioneer Honour for Bose', *The Telegraph – Calcutta*, 8 December 2008, viewed 28 March <*http://www.telegraphindia.com/1081208/jsp/nation/story_10221833.jsp*>.

Royal Government of Bhutan (RGoB) (1999) *Bhutan 2020, A Vision for Peace, Prosperity and Happiness*, Thailand: Keen Bangkok.

Runge, F.C. (1997) *Globalization and Sustainability: The machine in the global garden*, WP97–4, Canada: Center for International food and agricultural policy, University of Minnesota.

Schumpeter, J. (1942) *From Capitalism, Socialism and Democracy*, 1st edn, New York: Harper & Brothers.

Serrat, O. (2010) 'A Primer on Corporate Values', Asian Development Bank, viewed 20 July <*http://www.adb.org/ documents/information/knowledge-solutions/primer-on-corporate-values.pdf*>.

SHRI (2008) *SHRI Online Poll 2008*, Singapore: SHRI.

SHRI (2009) *Succeed or Sink: Depths and heights of business sustainability*, Singapore: SHRI.

Singapore Department of Statistics (2010) *Statistics: Latest Data*, viewed 12 November 2010 <*http://www.singstat .gov.sg/stats/latestdata.html*>.

Singapore Economic Development Board (SEDB) (2009) *The Best Business Environment in Asia*, viewed 12 November <*http://www.edb.gov.sg/edb/sg/en_uk/index/ why_singapore/dynamic_global_city.html*>.

Singapore Workforce Development Agency (2009) *Singapore Workforce Skills Qualifications*, viewed 15 May 2009 <*http://app2.wda.gov.sg/wsq/Common/homepage.aspx*>.

SKF (2010), 'Sustainability at SKF', viewed 18 May 2010 <*http://www.skf.com/portal/skf/home/sustainability?cont entId=508994&lang=en*>.

SPRING Singapore (2009) 'Performance Indicators', viewed 24 July 2009 <*http://www.spring.gov.sg/aboutus/pi/pages/ performance-indicators.aspx*>.

Stackhouse, M., McCann, D. P. and Roels, S. J. (1995) (eds) *On moral business: Classical and contemporary resources for ethics in economic life*, USA: Wm. B. Eerdmans Publishing, pp. 703–5.

Stangler, D. (2009) 'The Economic Future Just Happened', 9 June 2009, Ewing Marion Kauffman Foundation, viewed August 2010 <*http://www.kauffman.org/ uploadedFiles/the-economic-future-just-happened.pdf*>.

Taleb, Nassim (2009) 'Building a "Black Swan" Robust Society: David Cameron in Conversation with Nassim Taleb', London: Royal Society for the encouragement of Arts.

Tata Group (2010) 'Heritage', viewed 12 May 2010 <*http:// www.tata.com/aboutus/sub_index.aspx ?sectid=uZJCH0l2iwA=*>.

Teo, C.H. (2000) 'Education Towards the 21st Century – Singapore's Universities of Tomorrow', viewed 7 July 2008 <*http://www.moe.gov.sg/media/speeches/2000/ sp10012000.htm*>.

TME (2009) 'About TME Systems', viewed 15 May 2009 <*http://www.tmesystems.net/web/home.php?page_id=1*>.

Todd, P. and Bhopal, M. (2000) 'Multinational Corporations and Trade Union development in Malaysia', *Asia Pacific Business Review*, 6, Special Issue, 193–213.

Tracy, B. (2008) *Flight Plan: The Real Secret of Success*, USA: Readhow you want.

Travel Weekly (UK) (2009) 'Innovation is Crucial During the Recession', 27 March 2009, viewed 12 June 2010 <*http:// www.travelweekly.co.uk/Articles/2009/03/23/30548/ innovation-is-key-during-recession-awte-members-told .html*>.

UNESCO (1997) *Educating for a Sustainable Future: A Transdisciplinary Vision for Concerted Action*, UNESCO, para. 11.

United Nations Environment Programme (2004) 'Montreal Protocol, United Nations Environment Programme Ozone Secretariat', viewed 10 May 2009

<http://unep.org/ozone/Treaties_and_Ratification/2B_montreal_protocol.asp>.

US Small Business Administration (2010), viewed 12 June <http://www.sba.gov/>.

Vernon, R. (1966) 'International Investment and International Trade in the Product Cycle', *Quarterly Journal of Economics*, 80: 190–207.

Vernon, R. (1979) 'The Product Life Cycle Hypothesis in a New Industrial Environment', *Oxford Economic Papers*, 41(4), 255–67.

Wong, F.H.K. and Ee, T.H. (1971) *Education in Malaysia*, Singapore: Heinemann.

World Bank (2010) 'Doing Business 2011', viewed 12 November <http://www.doingbusiness.org/data/exploreeconomies/singapore>.

World Economic Forum (WEF) (2010) 'The Global Competitiveness Report 2009–2010', viewed 2 July 2010 <http://www.weforum.org/en/initiatives/gcp/Global%20Competitiveness%20Report/index.htm>.

Yeo, G. (2003) 'Singapore: The Global Schoolhouse', Speech by Minister for Trade and Industry, 16 August 2003, viewed 20 February 2008 <http://www.sedb.com/edbcorp/sg/en_uk/index/in_the_news/2003/20030/singapore_-_the_global.html>.

Yeung, H.W.C. (1994) 'Third World Multinationals Revisited: A Research Critique and Future Agenda', *Third World Quarterly* 15: 297–317.

Zhu, Y. and Fahey, S. (2000) 'The Challenges and Opportunities for the Trade Union in the Transition Era', in C. Rowley and J. Benson (eds.), *Globalisation and Labour in the Asia Pacific Region*, London: Frank Cass, 282–99.

Index

Printed in the United States
By Bookmasters